PELICAN

LAW AND
IN PERSP

Arthur Seldon was born in 1923 and educated in Wales. He graduated in social psychology and politics and after qualifying as an accountant he joined the civil service in the Department of Trade and Industry. He then read law and was later appointed an Official Receiver. For twenty years he was an officer of the courts in the south-west of England and he also acted as Deputy for the Official Receiver attached to the High Court of Justice. In 1983 he was invested a Companion of the Imperial Service Order.

London

Oct 25 87

ARTHUR SELDON

LAW AND LAWYERS
IN PERSPECTIVE

PENGUIN BOOKS

Penguin Books Ltd, Harmondsworth, Middlesex, England
Viking Penguin Inc., 40 West 23rd Street, New York, New York 10010, U.S.A.
Penguin Books Australia Ltd, Ringwood, Victoria, Australia
Penguin Books Canada Ltd, 2801 John Street, Markham, Ontario, Canada L3R 1B4
Penguin Books (N.Z.) Ltd, 182–190 Wairau Road, Auckland 10, New Zealand

First published 1987

Made and printed in Great Britain by
Richard Clay Ltd, Bungay, Suffolk
Typeset in Ehrhardt

CONTENTS

INTRODUCTION

The common law of England has been laboriously built up
about a mythical figure – the figure of the reasonable man.

A. P. HERBERT, *Uncommon Law* (1935)

This book is aimed neither at the student of law nor at those laymen
who wish to do their own legal work without the aid of professional
lawyers. There is an abundance of books that fulfil that purpose
written for lawyers both professional and amateur. The present work
is far less ambitious. Firstly, it is intended to be a compendium of the
observations and arguments of academics and professionals in various
fields of law – the rules of law, the police, the courts, juries, lawyers
and the treatment of offenders – collated to give a general picture of
the law of England and Wales as a whole, intelligible to those with
little experience of the law and enabling them to participate in the
current controversies concerning its administration. It is intended not
as a critique, but as an attempt to present a concise perspective of the
whole scenario of the law and its administration as it exists and
functions in society, situated at the meeting of the disciplines of
jurisprudence, social psychology and and sociology. In certain matters
it has been impossible to avoid suggestions on how things ought to be,
but they have been kept to a minimum and should not unduly influence the reader or prevent the achievement of the second aim of
the work, to dispel many common misconceptions concerning law.

Though they have tended to ignore the details of the legislation
and its operation, the British public has always shown a marked
political awareness of, and have been deeply concerned with, the
nature of legislation emanating from Parliament. Indeed, in most
instances defects in law become well known to the public long before
Parliament is aware of them and a change in law is brought about
only after considerable pressure by those affected by the defects, and
their supporters. But after the laws are on the statute book, the
majority of the population consider the application of law to be so

fraught with technicalities and complex procedures and are so awed
by legal ritual that they leave the whole machinery of enforcement to
lawyers. This should never be so. Lawyers are merely professional
men acting as agents in assisting their principals – their clients.
(This relationship is acknowledged by barristers and solicitors when
they are in difficulty in court proceedings and claim that 'they are
without instructions' or that 'they will have to obtain instructions'.)
Instead of acquiring a general knowledge of the operation of the law
and relying upon lawyers to assist them only in the detailed interpretation of Acts and procedures, the public has allowed lawyers,
when acting for them, virtually to take over their affairs, control the
legal system and create for themselves an elitist citadel within society
which they have shrouded in mystery and ritual. Because barristers
and solicitors have led the public to believe that they administer
justice and not merely apply the law, they have been highly successful
in local and parliamentary elections. They have become so well represented and influential in the House of Commons, the House of
Lords, the government and indeed the Cabinet itself that it could be
argued that they have become almost immune from official censure.

The legal profession claims that the judges and the courts in which
they operate are completely independent and free from influence,
political or otherwise, and they point to the Act of Settlement of
1700, and to later enactments in the middle of the nineteenth century
and in 1981, under which judges (who are at the apex of the legal
profession) cannot be removed or dismissed and their salary cannot
be reduced should they fail to please 'the King or the ministers
in power'. They assert that in a free society, whatever the duties
and obligations imposed upon the subject by the state or any other
authority, they should be enforceable only in a legal manner and on
legal authority. This is known as the Rule of Law, for the successful
operation of which the judiciary must be completely independent of
government. According to this argument the judges are completely
free and independent and are not accountable to any authority, not
even the community they serve.

The role of judges has been subject to a debate that has lasted for
many years. Some contend that they merely declare the law as it
exists, while others hold that they make judicial law by interpreting
principles in the light of new combinations of fact. There is indeed

an impressive and formidable body of opinion which supports the claim that judges make the law. If that opinion is correct, it is fundamentally wrong for a democratic state to have, as lawmakers, judges who are appointed by the executive and are thereafter independent and outside the control of any authority. If the opposing opinion is correct and the judges' role is to declare the law, they must exercise a choice between alternative interpretations, all of which may be legally justified. If this choice concerns industrial relations or other politically sensitive matters, it is highly probable that a conscious or unconscious political bias will permeate the decision. While this risk exists, and while judges are able to see themselves to be the ultimate interpreters of public good, as many do, they should be responsible, ultimately, to the community for the decisions they make on its behalf.

The Inns of Court (the barristers' professional bodies, the senior members of which are the judges) are entirely independent. The Law Society (the solicitors' professional body), although subject to legislative control, has been widely criticized because of the anomalous position it occupies. It is primarily a representative body for solicitors, financed by membership subscriptions from solicitors and, according to its rules, a democratic organization, the officers of which are elected by its members. Although it exercises a degree of discipline over its members and is subject to certain legal duties under the various Solicitors' Acts, it is essentially a body to further their interests. Indeed, there are wide fields of professional incompetence and negligence with which the Law Society is not concerned. Yet successive governments have permitted the Law Society to control the legal aid fund without the interference of laymen, thus allowing it to authorize its members to act on behalf of others and pay them for doing so from central government funds.

As a result of the criticisms of the activities of the Law Society, mainly from laymen adversely affected by it, in May 1984 it commissioned a firm of management consultants to carry out a major review of its structure, functions and organization, but of course the consultants could do nothing concerning the conflict of interest ostensibly imposed upon it by the government in placing the legal aid fund under its control, particularly in civil matters. This situation encourages solicitors to persuade legally aided persons to pursue hopeless claims to the bitter end. The client has nothing to lose and the solicitor all to gain in fees. In October 1984, the Master of the Rolls (the head of the Appeal Court), Sir John Donaldson, urged radical reforms in civil procedure, to reduce the long delays in civil cases coming before the courts. Among other things he suggested that the courts should have new powers to prevent litigation of claims that were bound to fail and to fine those who abused the court process by bringing claims in bad faith. He went on to suggest that a system was needed under which those who had legal rights to enforce or protect received better treatment, while those who did not and were unsuccessful in litigation had rather more at stake. Although he did not have it specifically in mind, the comments are particularly germane to legally assisted persons and their solicitors.

To dispel the misconceptions concerning the law and lawyers held by a large section of the community, each chapter of this work has been devoted to a specific facet of the law and its operation. Many believe that law is synonymous with justice, that English law is unique, with its origins firmly rooted in English history, and that the Rules of Legal Procedure constitute the Rule of Law. Some believe that police officers are incorruptible, independent and individual holders of public office, while others see them as prejudiced, corruptible, avaricious and functionaries of the privileged. Others believe the courts, judges and lawyers are the epitome of impartiality and arrive at faultless decisions. Yet others believe the jury is a peculiar English institution and that when a person has been found guilty by a jury, a life sentence passed by the judge means precisely what it says.

A far more general misconception held by a far wider proportion of the population appears to have been encouraged by novels and plays. The plot and counterplot of a detective thriller or murder mystery may revolve around an exciting pursuit that culminates in the discovery or capture of the wrongdoer. By implication, the villain has been brought to justice and that is the end of the matter. Consequently, many people cannot understand why, in real life, every person they believe to be breaking the law is not arrested immediately and promptly convicted, although their belief of a person's guilt is often based on newspaper reports. They fail to realize that before any charge can be formulated, by the state or by an individual, a specific and well-defined law must have been contravened. It is insufficient to say that an action of a person was 'unjust'. The whole investigation, including the collation of the evidence, must be filtered through the police or other law-enforcement agency. Only if there is sufficient evidence to convince a jury that a crime has been committed by the suspect, and that a prosecution is likely to be successful and is in the public interest, will a prosecution be instituted.

If those obstacles are overcome and prosecution proceedings ensue, the accused has a right to legal representation, and the duel between the lawyers for the prosecution and the lawers for the defence has a considerable influence on the outcome of the case. So also do the judge's predilections concerning the nature of the case before him and indeed the constitution of the jury.

As this work is intended primarily for the laity, it has not been burdened with an elaborate system of footnotes and references, but for those who may desire further readings on the subjects raised a select Bibliography has been appended.

I

LAW AND JUSTICE

A rape, a rape! . . .
Yes, you have ravished justice,
Forced her to do your pleasure.

JOHN WEBSTER, *The White Devil* (1612)

Law and justice are two entirely different concepts that various governments unintentionally confuse in their efforts to persuade their people that their laws are 'just'. The position is aggravated because lawyers worldwide claim that they administer not only the law but also justice. Consequently, many people believe that law is synonymous with justice, and an equally large section of the community who conceive law as one thing and justice as another find it difficult to differentiate between them. They have not been helped by philosophers, who have failed to agree on what constitutes justice and to define it in a manner acceptable to all. Clearly, it would be naïve to say, simply, that justice is fairness, that justice is the maintenance of right, the reward of virtue or the punishment of vice. Each of these suggestions demands an endless stream of further definitions. It is a somewhat easier task to explore the concept of law – to ascertain the unique characteristics of the law of England and Wales that are difficult to reconcile with any concept of justice.

Legal philosophers have endeavoured to explain or define the phenomenon of law in terms of its formal source in the state, its roots and origins in society, its effects upon society, its method of application and its relationship with the modern state. But at the same time, founders of religions and men of science, whose discoveries have transformed the human concept of the universe, have all from time to time referred to law, physical or otherwise, as the justification for their beliefs or discoveries. Although they each refer to the law in widely different senses, there appears to be a similarity in the language they use and the ways in which they deal with their theories of law that leads one to think that they are all unconsciously referring to the same fundamental concept. In modern times each profession has its own laws. The economist talks of economic laws, the army general of the laws of strategy, the physicist of the laws of gravity and so on, but it is difficult to determine what the essential similarities are that bind together the various uses of the term. It would be a lengthy process to review the polemic dissertations on the matter, but a general survey of the conclusions of many thinkers who have tried to establish the essential similarities seems to lead to the conclusion that the concept of law in whatever sphere it is applied always involves the concepts of order and compulsion. Pure physical laws establish order in a particular science or profession, and scientists and professional workers elucidate those laws for the benefit of mankind. Indeed, their professional status depends upon at least a rudimentary recognition of them. The degree of compulsion that is attached to laws establishes the degree of order in the respective science.

Order and compulsion are also essential elements of law relating to human conduct, but they are artificially created and are certainly not as universally applicable as physical laws. However, some progress can be made in understanding law if order is considered to be the logical outcome of law and compulsion.

Historically, it is impossible to determine when order over chaos was achieved in human dealings and relationships, but the observations of social scientists and exponents of anthropology have enabled us to discover that the concept of law in relation to human affairs is not confined to civilized peoples but is found, though often in grotesque forms, in primitive communities.

It is highly improbable, from what is known of primitive society, that order in human relationships and affairs proceeded from a voluntary perception of the rational advantages of order. Rather, it is far more likely that it was gradually brought about by the exercise of authority on the part of those 'superior' members of the community who by reason of their strength, their age or their intelligence found means to make their wishes known and forced or induced others to comply with them. It has been argued by those politically motivated that the birth of order in a particular locality came about as a result of the compulsion of economic necessity, but even if this were so, that order could be established only by those who were intelligent enough to recognize the economic advantage of that particular type of order and had the ability to impose it. Nevertheless, it must be conceded that the laws of people in different localities throughout the world differed considerably and, as laws in some areas were diametrically opposed to laws in others, those of any particular region could not be considered universally applicable or universally 'just'. As civilization advanced and human minds were profoundly stimulated by the discoveries of experimental science, it seemed to be accepted by many Britons that the universe with which humanity was acquainted existed by virtue of uniform sequences of phenomena, termed by scientists as 'laws'.

Attempts to draw the concepts of law together gave birth to the idea that law relating to human affairs consisted of rules in accordance with reason and nature. This in turn formed the basis of a variety of natural law theories. The theorists commenced their inquiries with Aristotle, who observed that some laws seemed to be common to all states, and went on to examine the whole body of philosophical and religious teachings concerning justice. The central notion to the natural law theories is that there are objective moral principles which depend on the essential nature of the universe and which can be discovered by reason, and that ordinary human law is truly law only in so far as it conforms to them. These principles of justice and morality constitute the natural law, which is valid of necessity, because the rules of human conduct are logically connected with truths concerning human nature. This connection, they maintain, enables man to ascertain the principles of natural law by reason and common sense.

The attractions of the theory are self-evident. Ordinary laws too often fall short of the ideal, and men have felt the need of an appeal to some higher standard. Just such a standard is provided by natural law. Indeed, in his *Summa Theologica* Aquinas contended that an unjust law is no law and natural justice appeared to be roughly synonymous with morality. The result of these thoughts in England was to elevate the idea of law in human affairs with its components order and compulsion from a mere exercise of power by the stronger over the weaker members of a society into the dignified position of a function necessary to the existence of the universe. However, the opinion that an unjust law is not a law cannot be sustained while a government has the power to enforce compliance with that law.

Most exponents of jurisprudence explain justice from an entirely different angle. They suggest, for example, that although the cruelties of Hitler's regime shocked the world they did not do so primarily on account of injustice. They say that rape is abhorrent, but the last description to be applied is that it is unjust. Injustice is rather a charge levelled against men or laws that treat some people more harshly than others in the same situation. For justice consists precisely in not singling a person out for special treatment – like cases alike, and fair and equal treatment to all.

They contend that justice operates at two different levels, 'distributive justice' and 'corrective justice'. The former works to ensure a fair division of social benefits and burdens among the members of the community. An example suggested is taxation, one of the citizen's most onerous burdens, which should in justice be fairly distributed, so that a statute taxing fair-haired people at double the rate of others would contravene this requirement. Distributive justice, then, seems to secure a balance or equilibrium among members of society. They go on to suggest that the balance can be upset, but at this point 'corrective justice' moves to remove the disequilibrium by forcing compensation, or to redress the balance of benefits and burdens in society.

Distributive justice is the concern primarily of those whose task it is to enact constitutions and codes and make new laws by legislation, these being the levels at which the division of social goals takes place. The function of the court is mainly that of applying justice in a corrective sense. In a just system of law they expect to find on the one hand rules aiming to procure an equality of distribution and on the other specific rules relating to the application of corrective justice by the courts. Ignoring the fact that the physical, psychological and emotional needs of people vary to such an extent that an equality of distribution of social treatment is impossible, various sections of the community see their interests in different directions, and therefore the basic assumption that justice is the equality of distribution of social burdens and benefits is erroneous. A law passed that everyone attaining the retirement age of sixty-five years should be put to death cannot be justice, as it is generally conceived, although it would be 'equality of distribution'.

As regards corrective justice, one would expect in a fair legal system procedural and other rules to afford each party an equal opportunity of presenting their cases and calling evidence and to prevent judicial prejudice in favour of either party. Further, all parties should be equal before the law, and the legal rights of each should be given equal protection by the courts. This entails that today's plaintiff and tomorrow's receive the same sort of hearing, in other words that the judges should mete out justice without fear or favour, without distinction between high and low, rich and poor and so on. This in turn entails that like cases be treated alike, as regards not only the hearing but the finding as well. If today's plaintiff is awarded damages because of the defendant's wrong, tomorrow's plaintiff should, in an identical situation, receive an identical award, otherwise the courts would be failing in their duty of giving each plaintiff's right equal protection. Likewise, if yesterday's prisoner in the dock was fined a certain amount, today's should for a similar offence be ordered to pay a similar amount. Major discrepancies in sentencing would be inequality before the law.

This requirement that cases be treated alike in this sense points away from the system whereby each case is decided on its merits. Such a system strikes a balance between interests without involving a balance between persons. It therefore appears that justice, as defined by equality of interest, is not the most desirable goal of law. Indeed, most people's conception of the law represents a basic conflict between two different needs, the need for uniformity and the need for flexibility. Uniformity is needed partly to provide certainty and predictability. Where rules of law are fixed and generalized, the citizen can plan his activities with a measure of certainty and predict the legal consequences of his action or behaviour. In some areas of law, such as contract and property, this need may outweigh all others, and fixed rules that work in some instances unfairly may be preferable to rules that are fairer but far less certain. Another advantage of uniformity is that it substitutes fixed rules for the arbitrary 'fiat' of the judge, for laws of government are preferable to those of men not simply because they are less uncertain but because they release the citizen from the mercy of other human beings. Yet another benefit is the stability which social order derives from uniform, unchanging and certain rules.

On the other hand there is need for flexibility. The existing rules may not provide for the exceptional case. Some measure of discretion, therefore, is valuable where circumstances alter cases. Sentencing is one activity where completely rigid rules, preventing the courts from giving weight to all the factors in the case, would be wholly inappropriate particularly when some amount of individualism is desirable. Furthermore, flexibility is necessary to enable the law to adapt itself to social change. As society alters, so do its needs, and a serviceable legal system must be able in its development to take account of new social, political and economic requirements. Given an unalterable system of law, the necessary changes can be brought about only by violence and upheaval. Law that is capable of adaptation, whether by legislation or judicial development, allows peaceful change. This reconciliation of stability with flexibility is a permanent problem in any legal system.

Neither the natural theorists nor those attempting to define law or justice in terms of distributive or corrective justice have brought us nearer a reconciliation between law and justice. Indeed, they have in certain respects tended to throw the concepts further apart without defining them.

The theorists have not concerned themselves with the identity of the lawmakers, and no evidence has been produced by them to refute the statement that laws are originated by the most powerful parties or groups in society imposing rules of conduct upon the whole community. In Britain the most powerful political party (that with an elected majority) forms a government which, through its parliamentary majority, enacts statutes, but that process of lawmaking is far too generalized to represent reality.

Although the most powerful parties legislate in accordance not with their conscious concepts of what is good law but with their interests, either real or apparent, they can do so only within their capacity to enforce the laws they attempt to impose. As most parties are not all-powerful, they must legislate with a degree of consensus with the remainder of the population. According to Hume, 'Though men be much governed by interest, yet even interest itself and all human affairs, are entirely governed by opinion' (*Essays*, Vol. 1, Essay 7). He implied that if those who have the power to make laws are solely and wholly influenced by the desire to promote their own personal and selfish interests, their view of their interests and their legislature must be determined by their opinions. If on the other hand the legislators have not absolute power, then the public must have some influence to further its own interest, and the development of law is governed by public opinion.

In Britain, it has been a very long time since there was autocratic rule, if indeed it ever existed. There has always appeared to have been a body of beliefs, convictions, sentiments, attitudes and firmly rooted prejudices that have been held by various groups concerning their own interests, and the opinions of those groups have directly and indirectly influenced the development of the law. They have not had the immediate effect of introducing new laws, partly because of the habitual conservatism among the most ardent reformers and leaders and partly because of the nature of British parliamentary government.

History has shown that a development of the law in England has often originated from a single thinker or school of thinkers, and while a belief or principle may eventually be accepted and become the common possession of the general public, it rarely happens that a widespread conviction has grown simultaneously among them. The initiative has usually come from a man or woman of originality or genius who is presented with or discovers a new concept and preaches it to his friends or puts it in writing. The friends or readers in their turn become impressed with its importance and its truth, and gradually a whole school accepts the new creed. Eventually the preachers of the concept make an impression upon the general public or upon a leading statesman or very eminent person, who is able to impress the public and thus win the support of the majority of the nation. By the time a change in the law is considered, however, the concept is out of date, because the beliefs that eventually gain a hold, so as to bring about a change in legislature, are generally beliefs created by thinkers or writers who exerted influence long before a change in the law takes place. Thus it often happens that an innovation is carried through at a time when the thinkers who supplied the arguments in favour of the change are long dead. Only in exceptional cases and under pressure of some crisis can British legislators be induced to carry out a broad principle to its logical conclusion at one stroke.

These long delays arise partly because the currents of opinion that influenced legislators gain force or volume only by degrees and are often checked or superseded by other currents of opinion and groups which wish to maintain the *status quo*. When eventually a change is decided on, it is carried into effect incrementally by legislators who act in the belief that any change is not a new law but merely an amendment to the existing law. This is because lawmaking in Britain is the work of men well advanced in years, who are governed by the sentiment of yesterday and acquired their convictions and prepossessions in their impressionable early manhood. They retain their early prejudices and modes of thinking and when late in life they take the mantle of legislators they work in accordance with the doctrines which were current at that time. Both Houses of Parliament have an inveterate preference for fragmentary and gradual change of law, and with very few exceptions it has been so throughout the centuries. As a result the law of England has a high degree of continuity and sudden breaks have been a rarity.

Public opinion is also often formed by the propaganda of powerful groups in society aimed not only at maintaining the *status quo* but at leading the public to believe that certain states of affairs exist when they do not. The most effective propaganda machines in Britain have been operated by governments during times of international hostilities, but no single section of society in Britain has been so successful as propagandists as the legal profession in representing themselves as specialists in 'justice'. Lawyers appear to have embarked on a programme to lead the laity to believe that they administer justice, not the law. This impression is reinforced by the names given to the various courts and officers of the courts. The lower criminal courts of England are presided over by Justices of the Peace, and the Lord Chief Justice and the Lord Justices of Appeal preside over the entire criminal division of the High Court. Indeed, the full name of the High Court is the 'High Court of Justice'. The Court of Appeal and the High Court were collectively known as the 'Supreme Court of Judicature', which is now abbreviated to 'Supreme Court' but continues to be concentrated in the building known as the 'Royal Courts of Justice'. Moreover, 'judicature' is defined in dictionaries as 'the administration of justice'.

In Scotland the High Court of Justiciary is held by the Lord Justice General, the Lord Justice Clerk or any one of the Lord

Commissioners of the Justiciary. Dictionaries also define justiciary as 'the administration of justice'.

The most poignant psychological persuasion that justice is administered in the law courts is the effigy of Justice above the Central Criminal Court in London. She is depicted as holding the scales of justice in one hand and a sword in the other.

The impact of these processes and the natural theories of law has had the most marked effect upon the English middle classes, particularly among those who have had little or no contact with the law. The majority of them hold English lawyers, and those who sit as judges, in awe, as the embodiment of all that is good and the epitome of impartiality. Politicians often make use of this reputation and attempt to resolve embarrassing situations by setting up a tribunal chaired by a judge. Thus the indiscretions and sometimes disastrous decisions of a Cabinet Minister can be made to appear individual failings rather than indiscretions or decisions of the political party of which he is a member. Judges or prominent senior barristers are often used to pacify Commonwealth subjects or to report 'impartially' on industrial disputes.

In addition, judges and practising lawyers are generally regarded by those not directly involved with them as outside, or at least above, the political sphere. This belief enables judges and counsels to advise or express opinions on certain matters with an assurance which lawyers abroad might envy. Indeed, counsel's opinion in some situations is accepted with quasi-judicial reverence, whatever its real value.

This misplaced opinion of the role of lawyers has enabled them to occupy an elitist position in English society. However, lawyers are trained in the law of the land, and they act and decide within the framework of that law and the rules of its application. German lawyers worked within the framework of Nazi laws in the 1930s and 1940s, and it is doubtful whether any other lawyers would have acted in a different way had their countries experienced similar circumstances. As the laws of England differ from the laws of Russia and the Eastern European Bloc countries, particularly in regard to property, and as English laws also differ from the laws of other western countries, and the laws of Christian countries differ from the laws of Moslem countries, there seems little justification for the unique reputation of English lawyers as impartial administrators of universal justice or for the elitist position they hold. It will be shown that they attained these advantages as a result of accidents in the historical development of the law itself. Their position was later ratified by informal rules that regulate the application of English laws, rules that in the main were framed by lawyers or their representative organizations. They accomplished this notwithstanding the fact that the laws of all nations are devised not to lay down rules of universal justice, but to enforce a rule of conduct desired by the most powerful group in the state, and the only restraint on that group is the limit of its power to enforce unpopular regulations.

2

THE ORIGINS OF THE
LAWS OF ENGLAND

Law is a bottomless pit.

DR ARBUTHNOT, *The History of John Bull* (1712)

In explaining the origins and historical development of the laws of England and Wales it is not intended in a work of this nature to refer to the development of particular laws or deal with the law, as many textbooks do, under generic headings, such as crimes against bodily security, crimes against property or reputation, family law, laws of real or chattel property, or the laws of contract and tort. As far as this work is concerned the two forms that now constitute modern law, and the most important division of law, are firstly the decisions and judgments of judges, known as common law and Equity, and secondly the enactment of statutes.

In modern times both forms of law are believed to have equal importance in the legal system, but in the second half of the twelfth century, long before any statute law had been created (except for the simple ordinances of the kings who reigned from 1066), the king's judges, both in Westminster and in the circuits of the shires, set out to administer the king's law without formal statements of the rules which they were to apply.

At the time, the study of Roman law was undergoing a great revival in the newly founded universities of western Europe, and in the absence of a statute book the judges looked to ancient Roman law, the *corpus juris civilis*, as their source of inspiration.

Consequently, English common law probably owes its striking characteristics to the weaving together of the customs of the English before they were disciplined by the Norman system, and the introduction of the concepts of Roman law. It was not the first time that English law had been influenced by Rome. The name Britain was known as far back as the days of Julius Caesar, when it was conquered by the ancient Romans and brought more or less effectively within the Roman system of government and civilization. But the high stage of culture established by the occupation was not maintained after the artificial support of Rome was withdrawn. Little is known of the fragments of Roman influence that survived, and while Anglo-Saxon customs are claimed to be the oldest monuments within the English legal system, it is impossible to establish whether those monuments were purely Anglo-Saxon customs or a compound of the customs of the native Briton and the Romanized Briton.

After the Norman invasion all exercise of political authority in England was derived from the strong and centralized monarchy set up by the Anglo-Norman kings in the eleventh century. With the exception of the decaying power of certain feudal nobles, until the middle of the thirteenth century the monarchs of the Anglo-Norman line exercised an authority which later went under the term Royal Prerogative because it was incomparably superior to the authority of any other person in the land. It would, however, be a mistake to suppose that the Anglo-Norman monarchy of the first two centuries was absolute in the sense that the king could do whatever he pleased without repercussions from the masses. Time and again after taking possession of his conquest, William of Normandy promised to his English subjects the 'laws that they were worthy of in King Edward the Confessor's day'.

Although a complete record of those laws appears never to have been drawn up, there can be no doubt that the great mass of Englishmen believed and held tenaciously to the belief that their ancient customs, many of which were solemnly inscribed in the Domesday Book and others expressly guaranteed by various charters of William's successors (all being implicitly adopted by the coronation oath of each succeeding king), provided an impenetrable, if somewhat vague, barrier beyond which the king's authority could not go.

Of course, notwithstanding the legal machinery that existed, the period following the Norman invasion was a tumultuous time for Britain. The conquest had led to a flood of adventurers both military and clerical (as civilians were described in those days). They were cruel, oppressive and quarrelsome, but had one great virtue: the civilians or clerks showed a genius and affection for documents and records. This was in contrast with the English hate of documentation, and consequently our knowledge of Anglo-Saxon customs is mainly due to Norman records of the time. Clearly, despite the introduction of new systems of law, the Norman barons could not be denied their rights as conquerors, implicit in the morality of the time, to take a handsome toll of the vanquished country. However, William was determined that their exactions or oppressions should not drive the native peasantry to revolt or despair and thus destroy the fruits of his conquest, or, by their private wars with one another, lay the country waste.

William and his successors, notably his son Henry and his great-grandson of the same name, did much more. They set up an elaborate system of courts of 'justice', both central and local, to enforce the royal rights against the royal vassals. William promised the English their own laws, and eventually after a long struggle the courts became a complete machinery not only for enforcing the 'pleas of the Crown' but also for deciding the 'common pleas' or pleas of the people. English legal history shows that William meant what he promised. He enabled the peasant, even in his lord's own court, to protest, with the support of the homage of his neighbours, that he, though a serf, was by no means a rightless slave, but a man who had been guaranteed his 'law' by the monarch of whom that lord was a vassal.

A major difficulty of the new courts and the main weakness of the old system was that English customs and traditions varied from place to place. This was a state of affairs intolerable to the orderly and methodical Norman officials, who set up the great system of royal courts. The judges were thus confronted with the task of enforcing a uniform system of law which was to be applied in localities the customs and traditions of which were completely unknown to them. Consequently, in the twelfth and thirteenth centuries, jury systems were introduced by which sworn bodies of men in a locality informed the king's representatives of the circumstances of a dispute. This afforded the king's judges an unrivalled opportunity to learn local customs. The system was not a native institution, as is commonly supposed, but a foreign introduction which for a long time was bitterly disliked by the English.

This was the origin of what is now – fallaciously, as we shall see – considered to be the division of labour between the judges and the jury – the judge declaring the law and the jury finding the facts. It must have had the effect of bringing to the minds of the judges a complete knowledge of the infinitely varying local customs of the realm. The judges might, of course, have continued to enforce the local customs, each in its own locality, but such a course would have been abhorrent to the representatives of a central government, which desired uniformity in administration. In some way the king's judges, in their periodic meetings in London between the circuits to hear cases in the king's central courts at Westminster, seem to have agreed among themselves upon a process of fusing the various local customs or traditions into a common or unified system applicable throughout the country – a common law. Thus the great strength of the Norman influence was the uniformity it brought throughout England. The system of periodic meetings of judges on circuits was continued during the period of the Assize Courts until 1971, when they were abolished, and it continued thereafter through the Crown Court system with the High Court judges making sojourns to the circuits.

Meanwhile the source of other medieval laws, that of the Church, or Canon law, was in a rudimentary state in Anglo–Saxon times. There was hardly a definite body of rules separate from other obligatory rules of conduct. It is noteworthy that before his conquest of England William paid for the sanction of the Papal blessing on his enterprise with a promise to allow the establishment of a separate system of ecclesiastical courts in England if it succeeded. The promise was faithfully redeemed when he ordered 'whoever should be accused of any offence against the "episcopal laws" should come to the place which the bishop should appoint and there answer for his offence and not according to the secular tribunals but according to the canons and episcopal laws, do right to God and his bishops'. There was a rapid organization of ecclesiastical courts from the humble tribunals of the archdeacon to the greater court of the bishop to the higher court of the archbishop and finally the august tribunal of the Pope himself. Canon law rapidly developed, largely on the model of Roman law, which gave dignity and efficiency to the 'Court Christians' which not only made them a real influence on the nation but aroused the jealousy of the secular judges. Quarrels between the two jurisdictions were frequent, one of the most famous being that of Henry II and Archbishop Thomas à Becket, which turned largely on this subject.

The Church courts exercised unquestioned authority in many matters of law even after the sixteenth–century Reformation. It was the civil war of the seventeenth century that broke their power, but even after that they continued to exercise authority until 1857, when their remaining power was finally transferred by Act of Parliament to the king's court. The bulk of the rules of the Church courts were taken over and applied by the new tribunals and must therefore be counted among the sources from which modern English law is derived.

One other body of law, known as the Law Merchant, which was not of native origin, contributed substantially to English law. It was a general body of customs that grew up among those engaged in European trading, whether by land or sea, for the regulation of differences and disputes between two or more of them. The foundation of these usages undoubtedly lay in the law of the old Roman Empire, whose fall had reduced western Europe to confusion. Although the elaborate Roman rules ceased to have legal force, even in the countries that had once formed part of the Roman Empire, they more or less continued as local customs. Gradually, the development of the various sea routes along the Atlantic coast and in the Mediterranean, the increased shipping in the Baltic and finally the opening of the great ocean routes in the fifteenth and sixteenth centuries afforded an increasing opportunity for the revision and development of new customary trading laws, which showed an increasingly maritime character (the Consolato del Mare for the Mediterranean, the Laws of Wisby for the Baltic and the Laws of Oléron for the Atlantic coastal trade are examples).

It was vital to the merchants that they should have a body of universal rules to protect them from the arbitrary and unfriendly treatment which they would otherwise receive in the national tribunals of the countries in which they did business. As they spent the greater part of their lives in strange countries, they knew well the dangers to which the jealousy and hatred of foreigners would expose them, unless they could appeal to special tribunals of their own which would administer universally acknowledged rules of commerce. They refused to visit a foreign town unless the burgesses would establish there a 'Court Merchant', in which, as a statute of the English Parliament put it in 1353, their affairs would be disposed of 'by the Law Merchant in all matters touching the staple, and not according to Common Law'. In many cases these courts were connected with the holding of fairs and markets, and the name commonly given to them in England was the Courts of Pie-powders (*Pieds Poudrés*), from the dusty feet of the strangers who attended them. It was granted by parliament in 1477 that 'to every one of the same fairs is of right pertaining a Court of Pie-powders'.

For centuries, therefore, the common law courts suffered the existence of quasi-foreign tribunals in their midst and the law that the latter administered could hardly be said to be part of English law. But the growing insistence of the state that they should absorb the whole business of administering justice in the land, so clearly manifested in the emasculation and ultimate destruction of the Church courts, finally extended to the courts of the Law Merchant. The way towards the absorption of the alien jurisdiction was paved at the beginning of the seventeenth century by the publication of Malyne's work *Lex Mercatoria*, which revealed to all lawyers the hitherto secret mysteries of bills of exchange, bills of lading, letters of credit, charter parties, rules of averaging loss, bottomry, respondentia bonds and numerous other matters of mercantile law. At the end of the eighteenth century, Lord Mansfield, a king's court judge, had sufficient enthusiasm and a sufficiently philosophic mind to undertake the greater task of absorbing into the common law such of the rules of the Law Merchant as were deemed consistent with the fundamental principles of English law. Commercial transactions then came within the purview of the king's courts, and the local tribunals disappeared other than for ceremonial traditions. The rules of the old commercial tribunals, although largely of foreign origin, are now unquestionably part of modern English law.

The fourth of the great sources of English law was 'Equity', a name given to a body of doctrine having a curious history and occupying an anomalous place in the theory of English law. Equity was never laid down by statute, although Acts of Parliament have both expressly and by implication recognized its existence. It was evolved mainly to supplement the deficiencies and to mitigate the application of other law. Towards the end of the thirteenth century it seems that the inventiveness of judges began to dry up. It may have been that the great race of judges from Glanville to Bracton who formulated the common law in the twelfth and thirteenth centuries was replaced by more timid successors in the fourteenth and fifteenth centuries. But most probably it was due to the increasing size of the government machinery, which was driving the judges, originally part of the king's personal retinue, away from the royal presence into remote quarters where they were no longer able to consult the king personally on novel issues but had to bear the consequences of steps taken on their own authority that might encroach on the royal authority. There were complaints that the stream of royal justice was dying, and the newly formed Parliament took up the grievance in the Statute of Westminster of 1285. It ordered the Chancellor to extend the scope of the law. This famous enactment was not without effect, for a whole new set of remedies was eventually added to the practice of common law. But still by the end of the fourteenth century common law failed to provide for many grievances. This may not have been because it did not recognize them as grievances, but because common law courts held in the circuits were terrorized by turbulent nobles or cheated by fraudulent practitioners. Consequently, the Chancellor could no longer content himself with acting on the powers of the Statute of 1285 but gave direct relief to suitors who complained of 'defect of justice'. Instead of applying for new writs under the Statute of 1285, more and more suitors presented informal petitions or 'Bills' to the Chancellor, praying him 'for God and in way of charity' to summon before him the person accused of causing the petitioner's grievance, 'and there examine him and, by the Chancellor's grace, cause remedy to be found for the petitioner'.

Under the strong hand of the Tudor monarchy the Chancellor's jurisdiction was restricted to filling the defects in common law and correcting abuses in the conduct of persons who resorted to it for fraudulent or oppressive purposes. It then came to be called 'Equity'.

One of the conspicuous differences between the Chancellor's Equity court and the common law courts was in the matter of procedure. Common law courts had worked out a very stiff and technical method of trying cases. This tendency, as already explained, centred around the employment of a jury to decide questions of fact. It has been suggested that juries in the Middle Ages were ignorant and not very intelligent. The Chancellor disregarded all the elaborate rules of the common law courts and dispensed with juries. If the Chancellor thought that a petition had a *prima facie* case, he issued a judicial summons to the accused person, bidding him to appear before our Lord the King in Chancery on such a day under a penalty (subpoena) to answer matters in the bill or petition. When the accused appeared, the Chancellor would subject him to a searching examination on oath. He would then issue a decree, ordering the parties to perform certain acts or refrain from certain acts, involving such matters as taking of accounts, examining documents or setting aside contracts, with the object of remedying the complaint. In the reign of James I it was provided that where the rules of the common law and the rules of Equity conflicted, the latter should prevail. However, Equity was frowned upon by some jurists, and John Selden (1584–1654) gibed, 'Equity is a roguish thing, for that it varies as the length of the Chancellor's foot.'

By the end of the seventeenth century the rules established by the early Chancellors had hardened into a body of legal doctrine. Obviously, while common law and Equity jurisdiction were exercised by different tribunals there was a risk of rivalry. Indeed common law will never admit inability to provide for a case otherwise unprovided for. Nevertheless Equity judges have again and again claimed the right to apply purported equitable maxims of conduct to new conditions.

The final source of English law is statute law. Although the wise men or elders of the Anglo-Saxon moots had 'deemed their dooms', which were the forerunners of the later decisions of the king's judges on circuit, statute-making did not become a regular practice until the establishment of Parliament in the thirteenth century, and even then for centuries the number of statutes enacted was very small. The volume of statutes increased as time went by. It was the original intention that all Acts passed by Parliament should be capable of being understood by an ordinary educated layman, who should be able to follow all the directions of the statute. In reality this is largely untrue, in that a 'Bill' or project containing a large number of controversial matters placed before Parliament has to run the gauntlet of hundreds of legislators, each anxious to contribute his item of improvement or criticism, while few of them possess the knowledge or ability to discern the logical connection of one part of the measure with the other, or know anything of the rest of the law of which the future statute is to be an integral part. It is obvious that those with the greater political power or greater influence have the greater say in the amendments and criticisms. It can be no surprise that a measure often emerges from Parliament in a condition that presents problems of interpretation – and is a source of substantial income – for the lawyers arguing the points. Inevitably these disputes can be adjusted only by the judges in the law courts. It is not very surprising therefore that judges, in interpreting statutes, must often depart from the strict rule of *litera legis* and resort to methods more complicated than dictionary methods for discovering what the letter of the law actually means. Centuries ago, they were assisted in their interpretation of the statutes by the maxim 'the old law, the mischief and the remedy' and they were afforded a valuable guide to those facts by the preambles or explanatory statements that were often prefixed to the operative parts of the statutes. Over a long period these have become more infrequent, and the judges are now left to draw their own conclusions on the general purpose of a statute. In doing so, however, they are prohibited from examining any of the discussions concerning the statute in the legislature that enacted it or from taking account of any of the public or private announcements of its framers concerning the effect which they intended the measure to produce. They are expected to consider the language of the statute as a whole and subordinate particular sections to the general purpose. They then have to consider whether the interpretation should be a logical or a literal one. A judge's interpretation of a statute could therefore be entirely different from what the legislators intended, and, as the judges do not live in a vacuum, their interpretations are often influenced by their own political, economic and social backgrounds.

British citizens' rights developed along political lines and were legally confirmed from time to time over the centuries. While the powerful Anglo-Norman monarchy had entrenched itself in the institutions and imagination of the country, at the end of the thirteenth century the creation of Parliament provided a barrier against the king's authority and was immensely strengthened by legislative activity over succeeding centuries. Nevertheless, it appears not to have been until the second half of the sixteenth century, in the thought-provoking days of the first Elizabeth, that the conception of England as a proprietary domain of the king (or queen), and of the people of England as his or her subjects, a subdued people, gave way before the wider conception of what we now call a state – a political society or nation. It seems that the now familiar word 'state' was not used in this sense before the reign of Elizabeth, when it became extremely popular with writers and politicians and undoubtedly indicated a broadening conception of politics as the concern of the whole community. Later one of the most conspicuous appearances of the word 'state' was in the title of the Council of State of the Cromwellian Protectorate, and that might well have been the cause of the word 'state' as well as its contemporary 'commonwealth' going out of fashion.

These salient movements in the history of English opinion arose because the essence of free government is that its subjects should have the rights and means of securing the exercise of their freedom. This restricted autocratic rule. It was argued by those advocating free government that, whatever duties may be imposed upon a subject by the state, those duties should be enforced only in a legal manner and on a legal authority. This was a most original and valuable guarantee of an Englishman's rights and is the real meaning of the Rule of Law (Lex is Rex).

The conflict between Lex and Rex was the great point at issue in the Ship-Money case of 1638. The Crown lawyers admitted that for centuries there had been a doctrine that taxes could be levied only by Act of Parliament, and that the doctrine was explicitly confirmed in more than one great constitutional charter. However, they stated that in this case there was a crisis which threatened the safety of the country, though they could not explain exactly how. They claimed that the king's word must be accepted, and that the levy of the tax could not be questioned. Rex is Lex.

Against this, advocates argued that the law of England was that no tax could be levied save under Act of Parliament and, as it was admitted that no such Act was passed, the claim for such a tax could not be enforced. Lex is Rex.

It was upon that issue that the Civil War was fought and Lex is Rex prevailed. The Rule of Law is buttressed by the famous and most valuable remedy of the Writ of Habeas Corpus. The writ has had a most curious history. It was apparently invented as far back as the twelfth century, for the purpose of putting accused persons in prison. Over the following centuries, it gradually became converted by the actions of the courts, into a means of rescuing persons from unlawful custody. In later years, by successive Acts of Parliament of 1640, 1679 and 1816, the remedy of Habeas Corpus was gradually perfected and made to extend to the unlawful imprisonment by all other private persons. Now it is a general remedy against unlawful imprisonment far more valuable than any other and is vital to the protection of the rights of the subject according to the law.

However, since political power was wrested from the monarchy, and Parliament became the centre of political power and supreme legislator, the protection of the subject afforded by the Rule of Law and Writ of Habeas Corpus relies upon the absolute independence of the judges from Parliament and the executive. If the judges were not independent those provisions could be ignored or implemented at the whim of their political masters.

3

THE RULES OF PROCEDURE

'I am not determining a point of law, I am restoring tranquillity.'

EDMUND BURKE, *Speech on Conciliation with America* (1775)

While, in common with the laws of other countries, English law has its defects, it is a matter of pride to Englishmen and women that people come from virtually all parts of the world to study what the English like to consider to be the working of English 'justice'. The majority do not come because of the virtues of English law or because they agree with it. They come to study the actual application of the law to the affairs of everyday life of the men and women of whom the community is composed. This is the supreme practical test of the virtue of a legal system. An ideal body of law is not of much practical use unless it is effectively applied. Indeed it might well be argued that an illogical and otherwise imperfect body of law effectively, dispassionately, honestly and humanely applied is of more value as an instrument of social peace and prosperity than an ideal body of law misapplied.

The actual process by which the application of the law is carried out in England is the operation of what are known as the Rules of Procedure. These comprise a body of regulations binding alike on all who resort to the courts for redress of grievances as well as those who preside at or practise in the courts. The rules, bulky and highly technical in character, although resting ultimately on parliamentary authority, are, in effect, the work of the judges, assisted by committees representative of both branches of the legal profession. In addition to these formal rules, there are a large number of so-called 'rules of etiquette' which mainly govern the conduct of legal proceedings. There is no precise penalty for a breach of these rules, but so strong are informal sanctions within the profession that offenders against them seldom have the opportunity to repeat the offence.

It would not be of particular value to attempt to summarize the Rules of Procedure – there are plenty of admirable works in which this is done in great detail. Rather it is proposed to bring out those salient and characteristic features of English legal procedure that have given to English administration of law its peculiar and indeed almost unique position in the civilized world.

Before any accused person is actually put to stand trial on a serious criminal charge, a preliminary inquiry must be held before a magistrate or magistrates, in order to establish whether there is a *prima facie* case against the accused. It is important to realize that this in no way corresponds to the preliminary examination of the accused, perhaps arrested on mere suspicion, which is common in continental procedure. On the contrary, an accused person cannot even be arrested, except in the case of flagrant delict, unless a magistrate's warrant has been obtained, and this can be granted only on information supported by oath. When the accused is brought before the magistrate, he can be asked no questions, but he can be represented by a lawyer who may cross-examine the prosecutor's witnesses. It is entirely the choice of the accused whether he puts forward any counter-evidence or merely 'reserves his defence' until the trial, and no unfavourable comment can be made on his decision.

Unless the evidence for the prosecution goes so far that the magistrates think there is reasonable probability that a jury might convict the accused, the latter is entitled to be discharged at once. On the other hand, if the magistrates think that on the sworn testimony before them there is a reasonable probability of the accused being convicted, they order the testimony of the witnesses to be put in writing and the accused is committed for trial. The important question that then arises is whether the accused should be allowed his liberty (allowed bail) or kept in prison during the interval that will necessarily elapse between the committal and the trial. Indeed, when an arrest has been made without a warrant, the police may release the defendant on bail, that is they may discharge him temporarily, subject to his entering into a recognizance, with or without sureties, for a reasonable sum of money, to appear in court or at a police station at an appointed time. Magistrates also have a discretion to grant bail, which they exercise according to well-defined principles. If bail is refused by the magistrates, the defendant is entitled to apply to a judge of the High Court, and he must be informed of this right.

The oppressive practice in some countries of keeping accused persons in custody without bringing them to trial has been avoided in England over the centuries by the famous Habeas Corpus Act of 1679 (already referred to), which provided that a person not brought to trial at the latest by the second assize after his committal should be entitled to be discharged from prison.

At this juncture it might be pointed out that minor offences do not involve the lengthy process of a preliminary inquiry and formal trial by jury. They are disposed of 'summarily' before two Justices of the Peace or a single stipendiary magistrate. The proceedings are commenced by a mere summons to appear, and only if this is ignored can the accused be arrested and brought forcibly to court. The case then proceeds with witnesses on each side being called, and the parties or their representatives have the right to address the court. The sentences that may be pronounced by the magistrates are very restricted.

It is one of the most conspicuous features of English law that all judicial proceedings are held in open court, with the exception of those concerning certain points of law or those relating to personal matters, which are heard 'in chambers' – that is in the judge's or Registrar's office. However, without exception all criminal trials are held in open court to which the public have free access, and the parties have a right to be represented and have their interests defended by skilled advisers in law from the Inns of Court or the Law Society.

This feature is accepted as commonplace by Englishmen, who may hardly realize its importance. The difference between the English system and those quite common in other countries where the proceedings are conducted in secret, and where in criminal cases the accused is not necessarily entitled to be represented by skilled advisers, is immense. The English system ensures that the enormous force of public opinion is brought to bear on the proceedings in court, and that judge and jury are compelled to hear both sides of the case. This has been the rule in England from time immemorial and only in rare instances, of which the notorious Court of Star Chamber is the most conspicuous, has the rule been violated. Indeed the unpopularity of the exceptions is the best proof of the value attached to the general rule.

The rule that every accused person may be represented by skilled advisers is by no means as old in English law as the rule of open administration of the law. Down to the end of the seventeenth century no counsel was allowed to appear on behalf of a person accused of a felony at the suit of the Crown except when a point of law arose for discussion. This was a grave blot on English justice. The first effort to remove it was due to the magnanimous attitude of William III on his consent to the Treason Act of 1695, which allowed persons accused of High Treason to be defended by counsel, but the rule was not made general until 1836.

It is also an essential principle of English criminal law that, with rare exceptions, a criminal trial can take place only in the presence of the accused, and the burden of proof in almost every case rests upon the accuser. That is to say, the person or persons making a charge that another has broken the law, whether in a criminal or in a civil case, must bring evidence to prove, or at least to raise a strong presumption of proof, that the accused was in fact guilty of the offence charged. It is not for the accused to prove his innocence, and if the accuser does not establish the guilt of the accused then the accused may, without offering any explanations of his own conduct, simply submit that there is no case against him and will thereupon be entitled, as a matter of course, to be discharged. He is not required, as in some other systems, to give an account of his actions in order to free himself from the charge. The mere fact that he is made to appear in court does not raise the slightest presumption in law that he is guilty. Hence the fundamental rule of England that every person is innocent until he or she has been proved guilty.

The only facts which may be taken into account in arriving at a decision of a case are the probative facts established during the proceedings. If the facts of the case are admitted by all the parties concerned, the matter becomes purely a question of law and evidence plays no part in it. But in the vast majority of cases which come before the court the settlement of disputed facts becomes a central issue for the jury. It is quite possible, although not likely, that in criminal proceedings the Crown may be able to call credible witnesses who actually saw the accused deliberately commit the offence for which he is charged, and the jury may believe the testimony. In that event, the accused is said to be convicted on direct evidence and such evidence is, undoubtedly, the most satisfactory that can be given.

However, criminals as a rule are not anxious to secure the presence of independent witnesses when they commit crimes. On the contrary, in a country in which the law is rigorously administered, they take care to cover up their tracks as carefully as possible and to conceal all traces of their activity. Consequently, in the great majority of cases which appear before British courts, the facts at issue have to be proved by indirect evidence, though of course the evidence tendered must be relevant to the issue. It is in a sense true that every fact and event are relevant to every other fact and event. The universe is so intimately connected in all its parts by the law of cause and effect that a complete account of the origin and existence of any fact would involve the tracing of an entire history. Obviously no court of law could do its work if the full implication of this reasoning was followed. Moreover it would not be easy for the legislature to lay down any general rule about the degree of relationship to the act in question that would make any fact proposed admissible evidence. As an inevitable consequence the judge is left very much alone in deciding the relevance of the evidence tendered.

There are, however, facts which may not be given in evidence. If a person is accused of a particular crime, evidence cannot be given, or admitted, to show that he had previously committed such offences. This may seem strange to the layman, but if such evidence was allowed it would imply that, because a person has once been found guilty of a particular offence, he must be presumed to have committed it again whenever he is accused of doing so. Again, no facts may be proved to show that the accused person is of general bad character, and the accused can never be asked during the proceedings whether he has ever been acquitted on a criminal charge. Manifestly, the guiding rule that excludes this type of evidence is apprehension that the accused might be prejudiced in the eyes of the jury and thus fail to secure an impartial trial.

On the question of relevancy it is facts and facts alone which can be evidence. Opinions are not evidence. Ordinary persons who rely upon their own judgments arrive at conclusions by a variety of methods. Following tradition is one of the most powerful influences, and equally powerful are a person's likes and dislikes. Common rumour or gossip profoundly influences many people's conclusions; they believe something to be true because everyone says it is. One of the striking characteristics of English law is that it rejects these patently wrong influences and in its investigation attempts to arrive at the truth. Needless to say, its methods are far from perfect and its conclusions sometimes mistaken. The search for truth is no easy task.

There are certain safeguards concerning the validity of the evidence given by witnesses. All relevant facts can be referred only in testimony given orally in open court. The publicity given to the trial provokes refutation if the evidence given is incorrect to the knowledge of other members of the public. The witness must take an oath or make a solemn affirmation that his or her evidence is the truth. If the witness then wilfully makes a false statement material to the proceedings, he or she will be guilty of perjury and be liable to a long term of imprisonment. The most exhaustive test of evidence given by a witness in a law court is that of cross-examination. That is to say, when witnesses have completed their own evidence by means of an examination conducted by their own counsel or the counsel of the person for whom he appears as witness, which is naturally administered in a friendly spirit, their opponent's counsel may ask them whatever questions he pleases, not only about their own evidence but about any fact relevant to the issue, however remote. Further than this, their opponent's counsel may examine them 'as to credit' with a view to showing that they are not credible witnesses. For this purpose counsel may ask them any question tending to throw discredit on their character or life, and they must answer such questions, on pain of being committed to prison for contempt of court if they refuse.

It is obvious that this power vested in his opponent's counsel must deter many a valuable witness from voluntarily coming forward with his testimony, but it has long been established that any litigant, whether in a criminal or a civil matter, can compel the attendance of any witness resident within the jurisdiction of the court by the simple process of handing him a copy of a subpoena or judicial summons, procurable as a matter of course. 'Conduct money' (sufficient travelling expenses) must be tendered. Unlike many systems of law, in the vast majority of cases, the British system leaves the weight of a witness's testimony to the discretion of the jury under the direction of the judge. This appears to have had far-reaching consequences.

Fortunately, with one or two conspicuous exceptions, England has avoided the ghastly error of applying torture to obtain confessions, and thus countless folk have been saved from suffering and injustice. If the tribunals whose history is free from the stain of torture are compared with the tribunals that laboured under it, the reasons for the difference become apparent. The common law courts used trial by jury; they did not use torture. The Court of Star Chamber and the Court of Chancery had no jury, and torture was used regularly in the former and occasionally in the latter. One can infer that the great benefit of the jury system, despite its imperfections, is that England was freer from the use of torture than other countries in the old world that had no jury system. It seems that a jury would not believe the testimony of a person from whom a confession had been extracted by the use of the rack or the thumbscrew.

Thus the rules provide that in all serious criminal cases the accused must be tried, not by the judge alone, but by a jury, and the judgment of the court must be delivered in public.

All criminal prosecutions are carried out in the name of the Crown and under the Prosecution of Offences Act 1985. All former 'police prosecutions' are instituted by the Crown Prosecutions Service, the head of which is the Director of Public Prosecutions. However, any person is entitled, on certain conditions, to use the name of the Crown for the purpose of conducting criminal proceedings, and consequently there are a large number of prosecutions for minor offences carried on by, and at the expense of, the parties interested in the alleged offences, either on personal grounds, or for motives of philanthropy or citizenship.

Another striking rule of English criminal procedure is that although the prosecution is taken in the name of the Crown, no accused person can be compelled to incriminate himself. This is the very opposite of the inquisitorial systems of many countries, the main object of which appears to be to extract an admission from the accused. In English criminal proceedings even the voluntary confessions or 'statements' of an accused person are received with the greatest caution, and any attempts on the part of zealous officials to entrap a suspected person into admissions of guilt are strongly dealt with by the court. Of course, a deliberate plea of 'Guilty' by an accused person at his trial, especially if put forward on legal advice, will not be refused, but the court is often reluctant to accept it in serious cases.

One of the most conspicuous differences between civil and criminal proceedings is that civil proceedings may be commenced without any previous or preliminary inquiry into the probability of the charges on which they are based being true. Broadly speaking, any person may begin civil proceedings against any other person without any precautions being taken to see whether or not his alleged grounds of action are frivolous and baseless. This feature of the civil process is due partly to the obvious fact that the accuser or plaintiff is not employing the formidable machinery at the disposal of the Crown but appears and acts in his own name and at his own risk. Clearly the necessity for a difference in criminal and civil law is rooted in the economic history of the country, but it is difficult to state precisely what the difference is in substance. The answer that readily presents itself is that any offence which in the opinion of the community deserves punishment, as distinct from the simple award of compensation to the injured party, should be regarded as criminal and be made the subject of criminal law. But when that proposition is examined it seems to be a very unsatisfactory one. The community's views on the object of or justification for punishment are constantly changing. Originally, it appears to have been regarded as a means of averting the wrath of heaven as an appeasement of the Gods from a community polluted with the offence. Later it successively appears as a process of gratifying the vengeance of the injured party and his kindred; as a sort of compensation to the community for the distress and shock caused by the offence; as a pure utilitarian means of preventing the repetition of the offence by striking terror into the minds of possible imitators; and finally as a means of reforming the offender.

This definition of civil law also fails on the ground that it is rare to find criminal cases in which the injured party should not be compensated. Indeed, in English law, some unlawful acts, such as assault, libel, burglary and housebreaking, embezzlement and many others including fraudulent trading by companies, are both crimes and civil offences and can be made the subject of both criminal prosecution and civil action. It has been suggested that the real distinction between criminal and civil offences is that, in the case of the former, the Crown has power to remit the penalties, while it has no power to waive the compensation due to the latter. That is in the main in accordance with the rules of English law, but it does not assist very much in the search for the true nature of criminal law. Blackstone, in his famous *Commentaries*, defined the essential nature of a crime in a few lines: 'to constitute a crime against human laws, there must be, first a vitious will; and secondly an unlawful act consequent on such vitious will'. He reflected the most influential legal thinking of his day and it is certain that, for a long time, English law clung to the view that every crime involved moral guilt of a substantial kind. Later, Mr Justice Cave said: 'At common law, an honest and reasonable belief in the existence of circumstances, which, if true, would make the act for which the prisoner is indicted an innocent (i.e. morally innocent) act, has always been held to be a good defence.' The immense increase in modern law of petty offences involving no serious moral guilt has altered profoundly the scope of the doctrine of '*mens rea*'.

It is apparent that crimes consist either of acts or of omissions, and for many centuries English criminal law, like all primitive systems, concerned itself mainly, if not exclusively, with criminal acts. The earliest known crimes in English law were murder, arson, rape, child stealing, burglary and the like, which were not merely acts, but acts that could hardly be committed thoughtlessly, in a moment of abstraction. Moreover, like all acts, they implied an intention, that is an anticipation of certain consequences and a belief or desire that the acts in question would or should produce them. As the consequences were flagrantly evil, the special form of intention necessary to produce them came to be called 'malice' or 'wickedness', and an accusation of malice was to be found in every criminal indictment. It may well have been put there rather to prejudice the jury against the accused than with any definite idea of the legal doctrine involved. Nevertheless it strengthened the theory that to incur liability for a crime the accused must have been guilty of some state of mind called 'malice'.

Criminal negligence presents entirely different problems. The offence is not an act, but the omission to perform an act, the duty to do what is imposed by criminal law. In most of such cases the accused pleaded in effect no '*mens rea*', but was defeated on the ground that he omitted to take reasonable precautions to avoid evil results. This naturally gives rise to the idea that 'negligence' is an immoral state of mind. But if the accused is charged purely and simply with the omission of a duty it might well be a good defence to claim that he had no guilty mind. Although decisions on common law charges are not entirely consistent, they seem to show that, generally, a conviction for a criminal omission is justified only where the accused has been guilty of at least gross carelessness. The accused could be convicted in any event if the offence was statutory and the words of the statute were so rigid that no escape was possible. However, most statutes provide that 'intent' is an essential ingredient of an offence when an act is necessary, and in the comparatively few statutes that create offences of criminal omissions, the criminal omission is nearly always described as 'wilful'.

Although the procedural rules and general principles built up over the centuries have been admired by many law specialists and politicians throughout the world, within the framework of the law and its rules and principles the opportunity exists for subtle influences to negate their effectiveness. It has already been mentioned that an independent judiciary is a prerequisite for the successful operation of the Rule of Law, but in addition law-enforcement officers, judges, members of the legal professions and the administrators of the courts must act with impartiality, free of prejudice and political or other influence, and every law must be rigorously enforced both in prosecution and in protection of the individual subject.

Unfortunately, these prerequisites do not always appear to be present in the English legal system.

4

THE POLICE

When constabulary duty's to be done
A policeman's lot is not a happy one.

W. S. GILBERT, Pirates of Penzance (1879)

The law-enforcing agencies are primarily the police and the law courts. Responsibility for the maintenance of order in Britain falls initially upon the police, whose job it is to bring wrongdoers before the courts. According to government publications, a policeman, whether a humble constable or the head of the largest police force in the country, is technically an independent and individual holder of a public office. He is the servant of neither his police authority nor central government; legally he is an agent of the law and it is his duty to prevent crime and to maintain the Queen's Peace. Whatever meaning one attaches to the word crime and whatever may constitute a breach of the peace, there exists in most states a whole body of law, breaches of which involve a penalty to be imposed by the criminal courts, and in England and Wales it is the policeman's duty to enforce all the laws of the country. In practice, however, the independence of the constable tends to be ignored in much thinking on the subject, and it therefore seems fair to refer to the conventional practice of considering the enforcement of law and public order as being a government responsibility carried out by the police as the government's agents.

Except for the Metropolitan Police, which is under the control of the Home Secretary, police forces throughout the country are controlled by their respective chief constables, who are responsible for the appointment, promotion and discipline of all ranks below deputy or assistant chief constable. They are, however, generally answerable to police authorities, such as a Police Committee or a Watch Committee of a local authority, on matters of efficiency and are required to submit a written annual report to them. The Home Secretary and the Secretary of State for Scotland, who have general responsibility for the preservation of law and order throughout Great Britain, are concerned in the overall organization of the police service and in its administration and operation. In this regard, they not only approve the appointment of a chief constable, but may require a police authority to retire him in the interests of efficiency, call for a report from him on any matters relating to the policing of his area or cause a local inquiry to be held. They are also empowered to make regulations concerning the government, administration and conditions of service in the police forces.

The Home Secretary is advised on all matters regarding police efficiency by Her Majesty's Chief Inspector of Constabulary and his inspectors. The inspectors are individually responsible for the inspection of forces and they must satisfy themselves that efficiency is being maintained by means of formal annual inspections of forces and informal visits and consultations when particular problems arise. The inspectors report to the Home Secretary on the conditions of all forces with the exception of the Metropolitan Police Force.

Up to 1986 the police were subject to what became known as the Judges' Rules, in effect instructions to the police, of an administrative nature, on how they should carry out their duties. The Rules appear to have originated in a letter dated 20 October 1906 from the then Lord Chief Justice, Lord Aberstone, in reply to a request for advice from the Chief Constable of Birmingham in connection with the cautioning of a prisoner. In a number of cases in the Birmingham area, the circuit judges had apparently criticized the police for not properly cautioning a prisoner when charged, and to clarify the matter the Chief Constable requested advice from the Lord Chief Justice. Later, over the years, a whole body of rules developed. They were not rules of law and it was claimed that they did not in any way control the activities or conduct of the police. However, it seems that they became so imperative that it was considered necessary to replace them with a statutory code of practice under the Police and Criminal Evidence Act 1984, which became operative in 1986. Thus while there is no formal link between the courts and the police, judges do have a certain influence over police activities.

Theoretically, all police forces and individual constables administer the decisions of others. They administer the laws equally rigorously and do not themselves make laws or rules, nor do they make decisions about the laws. This policy and duty of 'full enforcement' implies that the police are required and expected to enforce all criminal statutes and city ordinances at all times against all offenders. It suggests that the police are without authority to ignore violations, to warn offenders when a violation has occurred or do anything short of arresting the offender and place a charge against him or her for the specific crime committed.

Indeed, there are considerable pressures on the individual police officer to comply with the theoretical conception of his duties, because the clear-up rate of crimes is important within the police hierarchy and occupies a central place in the police value system. Thus, solving crime is a source of prestige within the police force and sometimes yields more tangible benefits such as promotion or transfer into the Criminal Investigations Department, which is generally believed to be a stepping-stone to promotion. This situation brings with it certain in-built risks, and senior police officers and the police authorities generally are most vigilant to ensure that the system does not encourage police officers to be over-zealous in their duties and endeavour to obtain successful prosecutions by foul means as well as fair. The authorities' vigilance is in the main effective, but very occasionally evidence comes to light that certain police officers have 'planted' evidence to obtain a conviction. These officers are rare exceptions to the rule, but they do bring a certain discredit to the force and enable many arrested criminals to allege in their defence that the evidence against them was 'planted', although that may be far from the truth.

At the other end of the scale, corruption, when it does exist, usually stems from the misuse of authority in exchange for personal gain. This is very difficult to investigate, but it is easier to do so if the regulations require that an officer should make an arrest or charge whenever a violation occurs. The officer who does not then do so is suspect. If, on the other hand, an officer is overtly told that his decision to act should depend on the circumstances, it would be difficult, if not impossible, to determine if his failure to act was an exercise of good judgment or was in exchange for a favour or bribe. If the exercise of discretion by policemen is authorized by the police authorities and senior officers and it becomes known to the criminal and the police officers concerned, it creates the atmosphere and affords a bargaining power for a corrupt act. Fear of this possibility is a strong reason why open acknowledgement of an individual police-man's discretionary authority is frowned upon by police authorities.

It cannot be over-emphasized that corrupt police officers appear to be extremely rare in Britain, and in fact the vast majority of British law-enforcement officers are diligent and conscientious public ser-vants. This is shown by the fact that they generally accept re-sponsibility for all the unsolved crimes that have been committed. A police officer does not point an accusing finger at the conditions in society that produce crime and criminals. Instead, whenever the publication of crime statistics indicates a rise in crime, particularly unsolved crime, he feels that his department has in some way failed.

There are considerable administrative advantages in the theory that all laws should be enforced and enforced with equal rigour, and it is not surprising that the government, the local police authorities and the police themselves claim that the theory is strictly complied with. Also, courts do not expect the police to pre-judge a case and therefore require all crimes that can be supported with evidence to be brought before them. However, this does not accord with actual practice. It could be argued that this is in the main due to cash restraints and the shortage of police. For instance, when public opinion demands that certain offences should be rigorously pursued, the concentration of resources needed to do so inevitably takes away resources required for the enforcement of other laws, and clearly somewhere a decision has to be made or has to emerge on the priority of laws. In normal police operations, except for certain overriding directions from the Home Office, the power to deploy police personnel in any given area, and the decision-making powers relating to it, are located in the police management structure, and somewhere within it there must be de-cisions made on which laws should have a low priority of enforcement, either in general or on specific occasions.

At a time of crisis – such as the disturbances in the miners' strike of 1984 – the police turn out in force, and large groups of them are transferred for short periods from their normal country locations to the scenes of the disturbances. Inevitably, their ability to enforce certain areas of law in their own locations is weakened.

Another area of police decision-making on law enforcement is whether or not a prosecution is likely to be successful if a matter is reported and a charge is brought against a known or suspected offender. It would be impractical and intolerable to report or prosecute cases other than those in which there is sufficient evidence collected with available resources to offer a good chance of conviction. If prosecutions were undertaken whenever there was the slightest evidence against a person, there would clearly be a waste of a vast amount of police time, judicial time and public money. It is extremely doubtful whether resources exist to support prosecutions on such a scale.

Indeed, to remove a large portion of the decisions concerning evidence and the likelihood of a prosecution being successful, the Prosecution of Offenders Act 1985 provided for a Crown Prosecutions Service under the Director of Public Prosecutions (DPP). The Act was intended to divert public hostility from the police by placing the responsibility for instituting proceedings with the Crown Prosecutions Service, though the Institute of Judicial Administration of Birmingham University feared that the new service would not be able to stand up to the police in deciding which cases should go for trial. In addition to those fears, section 8 of the Act provides that (subject to any regulations the Attorney General may make) the Chief Officer of any police authority is required to give information to the DPP concerning every matter 'which appears to the police chief, to be a *prima facie* case for proceedings'. Thus, in the majority of instances, a very large measure of discretion as to whether or not there is a *prima facie* case for proceedings remains with the police, and decisions as to which matters, information and statements should be referred to the Crown Prosecutions Service must of necessity remain with the police unless a blatant well-publicized offence has been committed.

There are proposals for the creation of a Serious Fraud Office operating under a Director who will be responsible for all cases of serious fraud and will have similar powers to the Director of Public Prosecutions. He will be empowered to carry out complex fraud investigations in conjunction with the police, institute any criminal proceedings that appear to be related to such fraud and to take over the conduct of any such proceedings at any stage. Thus police decision-making in connection with complex fraud matters will be considerably reduced.

In addition to the restrictions placed on total law enforcement by limited resources, the police experience difficulty in attempting total enforcement of the law while there remain a number of laws on the statute book which are obsolete, unsupported by public opinion, but have not been formally repealed. However, the ordinary policemen find themselves in far greater difficulty than in those circumstances already mentioned when the views of the public reveal widely conflicting opinions by different sections of the community concerning the way the police should deal with a problem that has arisen. This must inevitably subject police activity to the personal likes and dislikes of the policemen involved and such subjective attitudes give rise to endless possibilities of partiality and discrimination.

It must always be remembered that individual police officers are recruited from the general public, they are human beings and, like all human beings everywhere, they are influenced by the actions and views of those around them. People's perception of a situation and the actions involved have a profound structuring effect on their actions and it would be remarkable if this was not also so both with policemen and with those with whom they have to deal. The more often a particular crime is committed by members of a certain group in society, the more likely are the police to expect a similar crime to have been committed by a member of that group. This is inevitable in police work or indeed investigation work of any description.

When a crime is reported there are rarely any known suspects and anyone could have committed it. Individual policemen must have frames of reference (albeit unspoken ones) to guide them in the likely direction of the offender. It inevitably follows that the police come to expect certain types of behaviour from certain individuals or groups, though in most instances police stereotypes fit the popular view of the matter and in this sense could be said to reflect public opinion. Such images are not just one-way. The perceptions that other groups have of the police often reinforce the policemen's perception of them. Thus it happens that images that the police have of certain immigrants encourage the latter to adopt a hostile attitude to the police, which leads to a circle of self-reinforcing images. Furthermore, the views of some left-wing demonstrators that the police are lackeys of the wealthy and privileged lead them to take up a stance towards the police which is likely to fit in with the police stereotypes of them as 'out to make trouble'. It is most unlikely that a Salvation Army band and its followers on a street corner would be regarded in the same way by the police as an extreme political organization with precisely the same accoutrements, on the same site.

It cannot therefore be disputed that the police, at various levels from constable to chief constable, either alone or in concert with other officers, have of necessity a decision-making role to perform involving discretion in the enforcement of laws. However, the police themselves do not acknowledge the fact that they have any discretion, because that would belie the very image in which they take such pride and which they strive so hard to present – the image of objectivity, of impartiality and of enforcement without fear or favour. A cursory examination of the typical oath of office administered to police officers, the rules and regulations of the police departments and the code governing police conduct gives the general impression that strict adherence to the law has to be the ideal towards which all well-intentioned police officers should strive.

While emphasis is placed on the policeman's duties as a law-enforcement officer and the administrative advantages of the model, the ordinary police constable is also concerned with the maintenance of the peace, as a peace officer. This involves a conflict in the ideals of policing. Investigations have revealed that other duties occupy far more of a policeman's time than law enforcement. He responds to requests for assistance, and his duties include, among other things, attending the site of a turn-out by fire or ambulance brigades, delivering urgent messages from hospitals to the relatives of sick and dying patients, directing traffic at busy junctions and generally being available for other appeals for help. In this capacity, rural police constables, who have always been an essential part of rural society, have always been involved in some degree of discrimination in the enforcement of the law. In their aim to be 'peace officers' they have given many traffic offenders (in former days it was poachers) a word of advice on the spot rather than a summons and many an erring youngster an immediate admonition rather than dragging him into the juvenile court. Their 'peace-keeping' orientation to their duties is aimed at maintaining a 'quiet patch'. In recent years efforts have been made to reintroduce this orientation in urban areas by means of community policing, which involves keeping a uniformed officer in the same restricted area long enough for him to get to know the people living there and become part of the social structure. To enable him to do so he must be informally authorized to build up a bargaining counter as regards minor infringements, such as the right of caution or let-off, so that he can obtain an intimate knowledge of the area and its villains, and be able to obtain information on matters that require investigation by other law-enforcement officers in the police force.

This aspect of police work over the years has played a very important part in the maintenance of order in Britain, in that the ordinary police constable became the symbol of law and order in society. Unfortunately, in some industrial and political areas the police have come to be regarded as representatives of an oppressive government or oppressive management. As a result, industrial workers in the country have been attacking the police, who have had to break with tradition and resort to riot shields and other devices to protect themselves. It is a tragedy and quite alien to British styles of policing that it has been found necessary for a special section of riot police to be formed, with all the implications that entails. However, if the various factors referred to that tend to influence the police decision-making truly reflect the factors that influence the decision-making of the general public, one could say, despite the risks that may be present, that extreme opinions would tend to be cancelled out and the police would be fairly representative of the community. If, however, a large proportion of police officers were influenced in any one particular way, so as to believe, for instance, that a certain ethnic group were inherent wrong-doers, the entire police service could quite well be prejudiced.

This danger is recognized by the police authorities, as evidenced by the code of ethics issued by Scotland Yard's policy committee at the end of 1984. It asked all Freemasons in the Metropolitan Police to consider whether their membership of the organization was compatible with their duties to the service and to the public. The subject arose from an inquiry set up because of the allegations of Chief Inspector Brian Woolland, who was investigating corruption in Islington Council, North London. He learned that two suspects allegedly belonged to the same Masonic lodge as a number of senior officers in his squad. He therefore by-passed the senior officers concerned and submitted his report straight to the Director of Public Prosecutions. The Chief Inspector alleged that he was prevented from proceeding with his investigation and taken off the case. Later, when he returned from leave, he was transferred to the uniformed branch. Whatever the merits of this particular issue, according to Stephen Knight in his book *The Brotherhood: The Secret World of Freemasons*, published in 1983, more than sixty per cent of all police chiefs in Britain were Freemasons. Of the commanding officers of fifty-two forces in England, Scotland and Wales, he could identify with certainty only fourteen who were not Freemasons.

It is not suggested that membership of a society with royal patronage is wrong for a member of the public, but it certainly seems incompatible for law-enforcement officers to join a society that is technically illegal under the Unlawful Societies Act of 1779. Although that Act is considered to be obsolete, the police connection with Freemasonry has led to very serious accusations. Indeed, according to a former head of the Monmouthshire criminal investigation department in 1969, 'The insidious effect of Freemasonry among the police has to be experienced to be believed.'

In 1878 the entire detective department of Scotland Yard was disbanded after it was discovered that virtually every member was a Freemason and was involved in corruption with criminals who were also members of their Masonic lodges. It was also suggested that there is evidence to support the claim that the nineteenth-century Jack the Ripper murders were committed by a Freemason in accordance with Masonic ritual, but that it was concealed by the then Commissioner of Metropolitan Police, who was one of the foremost Freemasons of the day.

More recently it was revealed during the course of criminal proceedings that a Detective Chief Superintendent and several officers of what was quaintly termed the 'Pornography Squad' were all members of the same Masonic lodge as a number of pornographers. The pornographers required protection to carry out their nefarious business and they got it by paying over £100,000 a year in bribes to the police. After the Chief Superintendent and ten others were sentenced to between three and twelve years' imprisonment, it was alleged: 'It is fairly certain that the basis of a corrupt network, of the corrupt relationship between that particular group of police officers and those particular pornographers was either formed or developed within the Masonic lodge.'

It is fairly obvious to most people that membership of a Masonic lodge does not in itself lead to or encourage corruption. It can occur wherever there is a meeting of minds and interests. It could happen in any London club, in a public house or even in a church hall. Nevertheless, the main reason for a large number of people becoming Freemasons is the expectation that it may improve their career prospects, and it is not therefore the police alone who are well represented in the Masonic lodges but every branch of the legal profession. Indeed, the time has come when not only the police, but also members of the legal profession, and in particular those who preside at courts and tribunals, should consider whether their membership of the Freemasons is compatible with their duties to the service.

Inquiries into informal police procedure have also been made difficult by their strong colleague solidarity. The reason for this most often put forward by the lower ranks is the need for assistance in a fight. There is a basis for this in reality. An investigation in 1981/2 has shown that at least thirty-seven per cent of policemen had suffered injuries on duty at least once and were prevented from working for some time because of them. There must be a very much higher percentage who are injured less seriously. It is of course impossible to estimate how many injuries are prevented by colleagues coming to the aid of a policeman in trouble, but there can be no doubt about the psychological importance to officers of the certainty that assistance is at hand.

The power of the colleague group stems from their control of the upward channels of communication. Senior officers depend on the men for information about the work situation, and the men tell them only what they wish them to know. Effectively, they can prevent leaks of information about illicit activities of any kind by excluding certain men from the colleague group. Recruits are taught the standards of the group and are motivated to adhere to them even if they run directly counter to official formal teaching. These motivations are many: the recruits want to be accepted as policemen by the group and they also depend on the more experienced constables of the group in structured ways. In his report on a recruit a sergeant must say how well the recruit gets along with other constables. The recruit learns his work only by watching his older colleagues, and many instances of light-hearted banter and ridicule of over-zealous recruits have been observed, as well as the total exclusion from the group of a non-conforming recruit. The initiation of recruits into various malpractices is a gradual affair, and a high degree of respect is given to those with three specific qualities: (1) the ability to stand up well in a fight; (2) the ability to say things in court that are not quite true; and (3) the ability to keep quiet.

Even at senior divisional officer level there may be a crisis of conscience in matters of 'loyalty to my men versus loyalty to a principle' kind. If a senior officer remains loyal to a principle he may lose the respect and support of his men on whom he so strikingly depends.

Notwithstanding this strong colleague solidarity within the police force and the high percentage of senior officers who have social connections with each other, until 1986 complaints against the police were investigated by the police themselves. This gave rise to disquiet among the public and as a result the Police Complaints Authority was set up, comprising a chairman and at least eight other members. However, any complaint made against a police officer is first investigated by another police officer appointed by the head of the appropriate police force. Every effort is made by the investigating officer to resolve the matter informally and various indirect pressures may be brought to bear to do so. If he fails or the conduct complained of results in death or serious injury (defined in the Police and Criminal Evidence Act 1984 as 'a fracture, damage to an internal organ, impairment of a bodily function, a deep cut or a deep laceration') the complaint must be referred to the Police Complaints Authority. But there are many ways of ill-treating a suspect that give rise to a justifiable complaint but fall short of 'serious injury' as defined by the Act.

However, when a complaint has been referred to the Authority it can only approve the investigating officer appointed by the appropriate police force or require them to appoint some other suitable officer. The investigating officer must in due course submit a report of the result of his investigations to the Authority, which in turn must send copies of that report to the police officer complained of and the head of the police force of which he is an officer. Thus, although the 1984 Act gives the Authority oversight of the investigation, it does little to take the routine investigation of complaints against the police away from the police themselves.

The individual endeavouring to pursue his or her remedies by a civil action against the police is severely handicapped. All statements taken by the officers handling complaints against the police are available to the police solicitors in their preparations to defend a civil action arising from the complaint. Thus any statement made by the complainant would effectively reveal the basis of the claim and the names of the witnesses, leaving the police free to interview such witnesses. The relevant statements may be included in the solicitor's brief to counsel and may form the basis of cross-examination, but as the statements taken are subject to a 'public immunity' they cannot be produced in evidence before the judge and jury, and further the statements made by the police officer concerned are not available to the plaintiff in court. It follows that co-operation with an investigation of a complaint will give the police a substantial advantage in any civil action connected with the complaint.

Complaints may also concern policy matters, but the relevant Acts do not really acknowledge the necessity of providing the right to challenge police policy. In evidence before the Royal Commission on the police in 1962 the chief constables gave partial recognition to the fact that they were concerned with a whole range of decisions regarding enforcement policies in matters which vitally concern the public interest. The failure to provide an effective means of challenging police policies appears to be due to the usual optimistic assumption underlying many of our arrangements – that law and order is not political. Legal machinery, it is claimed, is both part of and yet separate from the machinery of politics and government. This somewhat peculiar belief relies upon the existence of a settled constitution and a stable society, but it tends to break down when the law is put into operation to enforce policies that are the subject of strong moral or political disagreements. The suffragette movement and nuclear disarmament demonstrations are examples. Indeed, it is parliamentary responses to problems of public order and security which in the twentieth century have placed in the hands of police officers, and other public officials, many discretionary and in a sense political powers.

In addition, the courts have been provided with an abundance of evidence, in various cases against police officers who have erred in their ways during the course of their duties, to support the fact that the police, from ordinary constable to chief constable, must make decisions on how the law should be enforced during the course of their duties, and it is equally evident that police discretion does exist at various levels within the police administration. Ignoring the influence of membership of outside organizations and colleague solidarity, the different factors involved in making such decisions may be at a relatively general level, as in the case of obsolete or controversial laws. The decision may be influenced by locally accepted norms and interactions or images and assumptions about crime and about different groups in society that policemen, like most of us, tend to possess.

These matters can influence policemen to behave in a certain way or at least act as constraints in making certain decisions of a particular nature impossible. Therefore, in the sphere of law and order, those who are ideally intended to administer the decisions of others do in fact make decisions themselves, and these can either directly or cumulatively amount to policy decisions.

5

THE INDEPENDENCE OF THE JUDICIARY

Courts and camps are the only places to learn the world in.

EARL OF CHESTERFIELD, *Letters to his Son* (1747)

It is with great pride that the British government, a large majority of the community and the entire legal profession led by the Law Lords assert that the judiciary in England is completely independent and free from all influence and political pressures. This assertion appears to be based on a famous clause in the Act of Settlement of 1700 which provides that 'Judges be made "*Quamdiu se bene gesserint*" and their salaries ascertained and established' – a provision that removed from them the fear of dismissal or reduction of salary if they should fail to please the king or the ministers in power. The provisions of the Act of Settlement were re-enacted and extended in the middle of the nineteenth century and also in 1981 by the Supreme Court Act. This, it is claimed, is essential for the operation of the Rule of Law in an impartial manner, but there is no real evidence that the judiciary has ever attained the degree of independence that it claims for itself. The early English judges were royal officers who were tax gatherers, but they were expected in a general way to look after the interests of the Crown in all its aspects, including the management of the royal estates, the supervision of local authorities and particularly the investigation of the numerous occurrences that gave rise to a claim by the Crown for fine, forfeiture, casualty (a special sort of tax) or other revenue. But in England even the powerful Anglo-Norman monarchs never claimed arbitrary power, but attempted to justify all their demands with reference to a law which supported them. In some cases the attempt was an embellishment of the proceedings, but others were based on chicane or verbal trickery. Even in such cases, the tacit admission of the necessity for a legal basis was an inevitable contribution to the Rule of Law.

The oldest and perhaps the most important class of disputes with which the early judges or royal officers had to deal gave rise to the name 'pleas of the Crown', which is the technical description of the most important class of judicial business which is now known as 'criminal'. In essence, it is that the Crown is claiming to impose a punishment or penalty upon an accused person for a breach of the law alleged to have been committed by him. In the wild justice of revenge, the avenger is accuser, witness, judge and executioner all in one, and it was a long time before English criminal proceedings were relieved of the stigma of criticism on this basis. At first the information on which a criminal charge was based most probably came from casual 'informers' who reported it to the sheriff, who laid it before a body of sworn indictors (or accusers). With the restriction on the activities of the sheriff, the Crown considered it necessary to appoint officers formally charged with the prosecution of offences; and thus the Crown became both prosecutor and judge. From Norman times the monarchy brought law directly into contact with the mass of Englishmen through a county system of administration (later known as the assize) and it became one of the firmest convictions of the old common law that the proper place for a trial of any serious offence against the law was the shire town of the county in which it was committed. These trials were held by the king's judges on circuit.

This system caused the authorities a great deal of trouble, because certain criminals chose to live on county boundaries committing crimes in one county and, when they knew there was a warrant for their arrest issued by one of the county's magistrates, fleeing to the neighbouring county where the issuing magistrate had no jurisdiction. This was one, though by no means the only, reason why London became, towards the end of the eighteenth century, such a favourite resort of criminals. London is a border city of Middlesex, Surrey, Kent and Essex. Hence, a person committing a crime in say the Strand, under the jurisdiction of Middlesex, could escape over the Westminster Bridge into Surrey and hence if necessary into Kent and later Essex.

Furthermore, London, as one of the most important ports in the world, was naturally the resort of a large number of mariners, traders and foreigners, many of whom had committed crimes on the high seas. As the high seas were not in the body of any county, the only

way by which these criminals could be put on trial was by assuming
that the high seas were in the parish of St Mary le Bow in Cheapside,
in the county of Middlesex. These appear to be the main reasons why
in 1834 the Central Criminal Court was set up by statute and lodged
in the Old Bailey (or keep) of Newgate Prison. The court consisted of
the Lord Chancellor, all the judges of the King's Bench Division of
the High Court (which is referred to later) and the Aldermen, Re-
corder, Common Sergeant and Judge of the Mayor's Court of the
City of London. The Central Criminal Court was not, as commonly
thought, a part of the High Court, but it exercised jurisdiction over
crimes committed in a large and densely populated area of no less
than four counties. Its jurisdiction could be extended in certain
periods of the year. The court could also try crimes committed on the
high seas or elsewhere abroad and hold trials of exceptional importance and difficulty. It is needless to add that the court had and
has unlimited jurisdiction and therefore no offence is too serious to
come before it. There was no right of appeal against its decisions, or
indeed against those of any criminal court, except an appeal from the
Petty Sessions to the Quarter Sessions, until the passing of the
Criminal Appeal Act 1907, which gave an absolute right of appeal on
a question of law and a qualified right on a question of fact.
Indeed, the King's Bench Division had no disciplinary or corrective
control over the Central Criminal Court.

The Queen's (formerly King's) Bench Division of the High Court
inherited the criminal jurisdiction of the ancient Court of King's
Bench, the tribunal which remained especially associated with the
person of the king after the 'Common Pleas' had been fixed by the
Magna Carta. As the intimate council of the king, against whose
peace every serious crime was assumed to have been committed, it
acquired an exceptional and supervisory control over all courts
exercising criminal jurisdiction in the king's name, as well as over
other jurisdictions.

In contrast to criminal proceedings, civil proceedings, as earlier
pointed out, involve disputes not between the Crown and its subject
but between two or more of the Crown's subjects. Civil law is much
older than criminal justice. Long before the king or the state had
entered the arena, peaceful means for the settlement of disputes

had developed in England, as in other countries. What is known of the Anglo-Saxon laws shows that the ancient moots were busily engaged in persuading people between whom disputes had arisen to 'stay the feud' and submit the problem to the ordered methods of primitive justice — the trial by ordeal etc. or the acceptance of the cattle fine in lieu of corporal vengeance. The Norman monarchs found these methods in force in England and, far from opposing them, they refused to set up rival procedures and argued that existing procedures should be followed in what were really private law suits. By the twelfth and thirteenth centuries the royal procedures proved to be, in the minds of most people, far superior in efficiency to the old-fashioned way of the local moots and so people began to bring their cases to the notice of the king's judges on their circuits and begged that they be decided by the new procedure. Initially, the judges regarded this as a nuisance, but it soon became apparent that it brought considerable advantages in the form of increased influence and a substantial increase in fees and emoluments. This brought a change of attitude, and in the thirteenth century the royal judges were steadily crushing out all rivals in the administration of justice. Thus, alongside the 'Pleas of the Crown', the pleas of the subject, or 'Common Pleas', came to be recognized as an important part of the royal prerogative of dispensing justice. This combination continued until the Great Charter enacted that 'common pleas shall no longer follow our Court, but shall be held in some certain place'. This was the origin of the classification of courts into criminal and civil courts, sometimes overlapping, but in the main clearly distinguishable.

The king's judges' circuits of the shires to administer law became known as the Assize Court system and it changed very little over the centuries. The judges of the King's Bench travelled on circuit, visiting and holding court in a certain number of shires on the outward journey and a certain number of other shires on the return journey to London. The unusual name 'King's Bench' is derived from the marble bench, nineteen feet long by three feet wide, which was situated on the south-east side of Westminster Hall and was used by the justices when in session and by the medieval kings at their coronation feasts. The room became known as the King's Bench Court. The King's Bench Division included the Court of the Exchequer and the Court of Common Pleas and they used the hall from the days of the Magna Carta until the Royal Court of Justice was opened in 1882.

The degree of ceremony attached to the appearances of the judges on circuit varied from county to county, but everywhere there remained the tradition of a 'court day', rivalling the fair or pageant in attracting crowds. However, this was only one facet of the criminal scene: as we have seen, all criminal proceedings were and still are initiated in the Magistrates' Courts and these minor courts are responsible for dealing with small infringements in a summary manner. They were originally established because local people were responsible for keeping the peace in their own locality. In rural areas there still remains the bench of Justices of the Peace, who are local laymen and women appointed theoretically by the Crown but in reality by the Lord Chancellor to act part-time and unpaid to perform numerous judicial functions, including presiding at Magistrates' Courts. As time went by, it was found that in the larger boroughs and main centres of population the type and quantity of cases requiring to be dealt with by the Magistrates' Courts were too complicated and too numerous to be dealt with in the traditional way, and it therefore became necessary to appoint stipendiary magistrates, who were qualified solicitors or barristers, engaged full-time on court work and, as their name implies, were paid a stipend.

Early in the fifteenth century, provision was made for the Justices of the Peace to meet quarterly to consider some of the more serious cases and the court became known as the Quarter Sessions, as distinct from the Magistrates' Courts, which became known as the Petty Sessions (both the terms Magistrates' Court and Petty Sessions are still in use, to the confusion of the laity). The jurisdiction of the Quarter Sessions covered all indictable offences, but it was left to them to remit the more difficult cases to the Assize Courts. The justices in the Quarter Sessions were laymen empowered to pass sentences for alleged capital offences that were irreversible, for instance death sentences. It was therefore possible for an offender to be tried before a jury of laymen and sentenced by a layman who had little knowledge of the laws of evidence. To overcome the problem the Lord Chancellor appointed part-time chairmen of the Quarter Sessions known as Recorders (in borough sessions), who were drawn from the experienced ranks of the Bar. (The power of the sessions to elect unqualified chairmen was not removed until the Criminal Justice Administration Act 1962.)

After the Second World War and particularly after the introduction of legal aid (a subject to be dealt with in later chapters) the Quarter Sessions and Assize Courts were unable to deal with the vast volume of work falling upon them. There were often only one or two judges taking an Assize Court, and as the criminal calendar got longer, in the main owing to the increased volume of defended cases resulting from the introduction of legal aid, there was no time for civil business. This was so because there was one cardinal principle accepted throughout the legal system – that priority had to be given to criminal cases. Dates were fixed for the hearing of civil cases, and witnesses, jurors, solicitors and counsels were kept waiting very often for days, until eventually their cases could not be heard because of the pressure of criminal business. Therefore in civil cases it was frequently expedient to compromise a settlement between parties, and very often the compromises had little resemblance to the law that could have been administered if there had been a court available. Further, because the judges of the Assize were available in the locality for a limited period it was extremely difficult to arrange the hearing of long criminal cases without disrupting the whole Assize.

The Quarter Sessions were no better. They were presided over by part-time barristers, most of whom practised at the Bar and were engaged as advocates on High Court work. They tended to hold the Quarter Sessions courts during the time the High Court (referred to below) was on vacation, so that they could devote their time to their private practice in term time. This resulted in severe bunching in the Quarter Sessions that overloaded the system of service. In addition the part-time chairmen could rarely commit themselves in advance to extended sittings without great difficulty to themselves. As a result there was a tendency to commit long cases to the Assize, thus further exacerbating the difficulties of the Assize Courts.

During this period the civil courts developed in an extremely fragmented manner. Although the County Courts were established in 1846 to replace the old Debtors' Courts, in that year there were over two hundred ancient civil courts and tribunals exercising independent jurisdiction. The judges of the courts were of different ranks and were appointed to decide different classes of cases, with the result that there was rivalry, jealousy and overlapping between them, with unfortunate consequences for the suitor. After considerable effort, the Supreme Court of Judicature Act 1875 consolidated all the various nineteen 'superior' royal courts into one homogeneous tribunal, the High Court of Justice, now the one superior court of universal juris-diction of first instance in civil cases throughout the realm. Any court proceedings, of whatever kind, which are really in the nature of litigation between citizen and citizen could start in this court, which at the time was divided into the Chancery Division, the King's Bench Division and the Probate and Admiralty Division. There was also the Divisional Court, which comprised judges drawn for the King's Bench Division to hear appeals under statute on points of law generally, and the Appeal Court. The Lord Chancellor, whose appointment was political and who was himself a politician, was an officer of the court. In addition to being president of the Chancery Division he was also head of the judiciary. The Lord Chief Justice presided over the King's Bench Division, the Master of the Rolls was president of the Court of Appeal, but there was no particular title for the president of the Probate and Admiralty Division. All the judges in all Divisions are now legally capable of hearing any civil case which can come before any Division of the court and of exercising any power formerly exercisable by any of the courts absorbed into it.

While the civil courts were reorganized, combined and placed on a more effective basis, nothing was done for the criminal courts. By the 1950s the Quarter Sessions and the Assize Courts were experiencing the greatest difficulty in attempting to deal with the vast volume of work, which was far beyond their capabilities. In Liverpool, Man-chester and South Lancashire the volume of crime overwhelmed the courts and they were unable to cope. As a result in 1956, as an expediency, new courts known as Crown Courts were established in Liverpool and Manchester which effectively combined the Quarter Sessions in the area with the Assize Courts. Additional judges were appointed, and the part-time chairmen of the Quarter Sessions and the Recorders sat in the new Crown Court, as did the visiting High Court judge. The more serious categories of offences were left to the latter. Generally, the position did not improve, and in 1966 a Royal Commission on the Assize and Quarter Sessions was set up. The terms of reference were restricted, and the Commission was unable to consider the legal system as a whole. Within the parameters imposed upon it, its inquiries were thorough, and it appears to have been impressed with the more efficient operation of the Crown Courts of Manchester and Liverpool in dealing with cases in those areas. It therefore recommended that the Quarter Sessions, the Crown Courts of Manchester and Liverpool, the Central Criminal Court and the Assize Courts should be merged into one criminal court, to be known as the Crown Court. It was recommended that there should be full-time circuit judges interchangeable with existing County Court judges and that the Assize practice of visiting High Court judges should be retained in the new system. They also recommended that the few minor courts existing outside the County Court and High Court, namely the Tolzy Court of Bristol, the Mayor's Court of the City of London and the Liverpool Court of Passage, should be abolished.

The main recommendations of the Royal Commission 1966–9 were implemented by the Courts Act 1971. The Assize Courts were abolished and the Supreme Court was extended to comprise the Appeal Court, the High Court and the Crown Courts that were established under the Act. The existing chairmen of the Quarter Sessions, Recorders and County Court judges were appointed circuit judges of the Crown Court, and the High Court judges were to continue to sit in the main centres (see page 162).

At this juncture it is important to define the context in which the word 'administration' is to be used. It has two distinct meanings. The administration (dispensation) of the sacraments, for instance, is entirely different from the administration (management) of a business. Both meanings are applicable to law, but with entirely different connotations. The judges administer the law, but the Court Administrator also administers the law in that he manages the courts, arranges the judges' sittings and arranges and manages the court buildings and support staff. So far, the word 'administration' has been used in the context of dispensation, and so to avoid confusion the control and administration of the law courts will now be referred to as 'management'.

From their historical development it is clear that the operation of the law courts was the cumulative result of a combination of expediencies implemented from time to time over the centuries as the legal system evolved. Although the County Courts were established in

1846 there was no real attempt to rationalize the civil courts until 1875, by which time they were in complete chaos. The establishment of the High Court improved the situation, and gradually over the ensuing years all effective jurisdiction in disputes between citizens was exercised by judges appointed by the Crown in the High Court of Justice and the County Courts. In the County Courts, the judges, the Registrars (who were legally qualified people who undertook judicial decisions and who were responsible to the judges for the efficiency of the management of the courts) and the court support staff were all appointed by the Lord Chancellor, a politician. They were paid by the Lord Chancellor's Department (a department of the executive) and there was line control of the support staff by the County Courts Division of the Lord Chancellor's Department. All court fees were payable to the Lord Chancellor's Department and they were appropriated towards the costs of operating the court. The management of the County Courts was therefore without pretension of independence under the control of an executive department of government.

It was not until the Royal Commission on Assize and Quarter Sessions of 1966–9 that any serious attempt was made to provide a comprehensive management procedure for the criminal courts. Up to that time it had been extremely fragmented and numerous authorities were responsible for different aspects of it in the same court. On the surface the various courts appear to have been administratively self-contained units and there was no pattern or uniform control. It was suggested that the only one overriding consideration that influenced this development was that the court should be entirely independent in management and in the application of the law, but such haphazard organizational arrangements appear to have indicated a lack of organizational ability by lawyers generally and the reluctance of the executive to impose a logical formal structure. It was fortunate that the Royal Commission on Assize and Quarter Sessions of 1966–9 was chaired by an able administrator and manager, Lord Beeching. He had with him two other leaders of industry, a president of a trade union and a permanent civil servant. These were a counterbalance to the other members of the Commission, who were lawyers. As far as they went, the Commission's recommendations were sound, but its terms of reference were restricted to the Assize Courts and the

Quarter Sessions, which effectively prevented it from reviewing the legal system as a whole or recommending a management structure that would ensure that the courts remained entirely independent of the executive. Indeed, their terms of reference left the greater part of the legal system, the Magistrates' Courts and the High Court of Justice virtually untouched and outside the scope of their inquiries. They found that while the chairmen of the Quarter Sessions were appointed by the Lord Chancellor, they were in fact paid by the local authority. The local authority was responsible for the appointment and paying of the clerks of the court, including the support staff, who were sometimes local authority officers who divided their time between the Quarter Sessions and the work of their own council. Not only was the Lord Chancellor and the local authority involved, but the Home Office paid the local authority support grants in respect of the expenses involved.

They found that while the Quarter Sessions and the Assize Courts ran in harness, the whole of the support staff of the Assize Courts was at the High Court in London, but in certain civil cases the support staff work was carried out at the District Registries of the High Court in the County Courts throughout the country. The clerk of the Assize and his assistants and the judge's clerk and the judge's retinue on circuit were appointed by the Lord Chief Justice and paid by the Exchequer. The courts were provided by the various local authorities, mainly the County Councils, and as local authorities provided the judge's lodgings, numerous Mayors and Lord Mayors were cast out of the mansion houses to accommodate them.

Even after 1956, when Crown Courts were introduced in the Merseyside area, no steps were taken to improve the managerial system. The judges and Recorders were appointed by the Lord Chancellor and their salaries were paid jointly by the Liverpool and Manchester City Councils. The support staff were appointed some by the Lord Chief Justice, some by the Lord Chancellor and some jointly by the Liverpool and Manchester City Councils. In order that the adopted recommendations of the Royal Commission could be implemented, Section 4 of the Courts Act 1971 granted the Lord Chancellor the necessary powers to set up a unified management procedure for the criminal courts, excluding Magistrates' Courts.

Accordingly, the Lord Chancellor's Department chose field management for the seven circuits based on the local chief executive model and each of the seven circuits was subdivided into three or four court centres. Each centre comprised a first-tier court – a Crown Court with a Court Administrator (manager) – and second- and third-tier courts. First-tier courts are criminal and civil courts with High Court judges and circuit judges presiding. Second-tier courts are criminal courts only, with High Court judges and circuit judges. Third-tier courts are criminal courts dealing with less serious cases and presided over by circuit judges only. The first-tier courts are usually situated in county towns and the second- and third-tier courts are spread throughout the less important towns within the county. The Circuit Administrator was given general responsibility for the efficient operation of the circuit under the directions or formal policy on management matters from the Lord Chancellor's Department. Subject to the directions and the limit of resources the Circuit Administrator is responsible for the co-ordination of the subordinate staff, the conduct of personnel management and the provision of adequate court buildings and offices. He is also responsible for the allocation of the court buildings and, within certain limits, the allocation of circuit judges to the various courts. Under him the Court Administrators were appointed to courts or groups of courts within the circuit (see page 161). The line management responsibility from support staff to courts administrator and Circuit Administrator to the Lord Chancellor's Department is complemented by functional links within the judicature particularly at court level, where the Registrars of the County Courts and Clerks of the Crown Courts act as liaison officers between the judges and the support staff. They are legally qualified persons who are responsible to the judges for the efficiency of the service rendered by the support staff, and they assist the support staff on legal matters or complications with which they are not familiar. In the Lord Chancellor's Department the County Courts Branch was absorbed in the Courts Business Branch together with the new Crown Courts, and a new Management Services Branch was created under an assistant secretary.

Although the English criminal system was originally under the direct control of the king, this was the first time that the management of the criminal courts became the responsibility of the executive. The various local authorities remained responsible for providing the

Magistrates' Court buildings and they are responsible for their maintenance. They are also responsible for the expenses of running the courts, including the provision of the magistrates' clerks and support staff. A large percentage of the expenditure is reimbursed by a Home Office grant. The Home Secretary arranges for the audit of the accounts relating to Magistrates' Courts through the Lord Chancellor's Department, so that the actual appointment of auditors is the responsibility of the Lord Chancellor. It is extremely difficult to find any logical argument in support of this procedure or for the pretence that Magistrates' Courts are not under the control of central government departments. Another disturbing feature is that Justices of the Peace who preside in Magistrates' Courts fill one third of the places on police authorities and Watch Committees. Thus they have an influence on policy regarding prosecutions and afterwards preside at courts where the issues they have influenced are being tried.

The last and most important court to be considered from a managerial point of view is the High Court of Justice. The management of the courts and the availability of buildings are the responsibility of the Lord Chancellor's Department, as is the recruitment of the support staff. The Lord Chancellor's Department also has at least an indirect influence on the career prospects of the support staff. However, section 104 of the Supreme Court of Judicature (Consolidation) Act 1925 placed the support staff of the central office of the Supreme Court under the control of the Queen's Bench Masters. The Queen's Bench Masters therefore argued before the 1966–9 Royal Commission that the staff of the court was placed by Parliament under the control of the court itself and not of any department of the executive, and they were keen to point out that, under section 118(1) of the Act, the staff of the central office were officers of justice although they did not exercise judicial discretion and were deemed to be civil servants only for the purpose of salary and pension. They strenuously contended that that policy was right and they opposed all proposals for change on the grounds that such changes would be contrary to the long-established constitutional and traditional position by which judges, the courts and their officers are independent of government. Their argument was acknowledged in the Supreme Court Act of 1981. Nevertheless, the management of the courts, particularly the criminal courts, the court buildings, the appointment of support staff and the career prospects of the court staff became entirely the responsibility of the Lord Chancellor's Department.

Logically, the arguments of the Queen's Bench Masters that the judicature should be entirely independent cannot be disputed. However, as the legal system is managed by the executive and the only independence, in practice, granted to the judges is that under the Act of Settlement 1700 and the various Acts that flowed from it, there is considerable room for manoeuvre by the executive to influence the outcome of cases in timing various court sittings so that a particular judge will preside at a particular trial.

6

JUDGES

You wags that judge by rote, and damn by rule.

THOMAS OTWAY, *Titus and Berenice* (1677)

The judges who preside in the various courts are not really part of the community they serve. The judges of the High Court, for instance, who are at the apex of this elitist profession, are in the main drawn from the upper middle class, are educated at public schools and are graduates of Oxford, Cambridge or, in a few cases, London Universities. The circuit judges come from similar backgrounds, although more of them were educated in grammar schools and attended provincial universities. Nevertheless, a high proportion of the circuit judges are Oxford graduates. Judges of the High Court went directly from public school to university and thereafter their preparation for the Bar examinations was restricted to the meticulous learning of legal rules and precedents, and their pupillage in a barrister's chambers comprised a conservative legal training during which time the traditions and skills of the Bar were passed on to them. When they eventually commenced to practise as juniors, their work was extremely time-consuming and they had little opportunity for wider reading or extensive social contacts. Indeed, shields against such contacts were built around them. They were protected from intimate contact with lay clients by the intervention of solicitors, who sifted the papers and statements to select the points which might be relevant to litigation, and who attended all conferences. As pupils they would have been advised to make their friends among other barristers. Consequently they nearly always lunched in an Inn of Court with fellow-barristers and when appointed to the bench of the Inn they had more dinners in an ever-narrowing legal social circle. When eventually they were appointed High Court judges they were isolated from and insulated against real life. The court procedure is wrapped in ceremonial designed to maintain respect for the awesome majesty of the courts and the feeling of elitism of the judges. The robes, the wigs, the dog Latin phrases, the elaborate bowing and the formalistic procedures all serve to alienate the court and the judges from mere mortals.

J. B. Priestley, writing in the *New Statesman* in 1962, observed that the sort of conduct that curates and elderly maiden ladies now dismiss with a smile still sets the wigs quivering and the robes trembling. Much earlier, Somerset Maugham, himself of a legal family, wrote: 'his Lordship at the Old Bailey has a packet of toilet paper put upon his desk instead of a nosegay of flowers to remind him that he is but a man like the rest of us'. Nothing has changed since.

In *Lawyers and the Courts* (1967), B. Abel-Smith and R. Stevens commented: 'England has its normal quota of success stories from rags to riches, its millionaires who started as office boys, its tycoons who sold newspapers on street corners. But no one other than a gentleman, in the class sense of the word, has ever graced the High Court Bench. Working-class origins are not recommended for anyone with judicial ambitions.' This generalization is not strictly true, but surveys carried out appear to confirm the tendency and it is exceptional to find deviations from that pattern. An analysis published by the *Economist* in 1956 of members of the Judicial Committee of the Privy Council – that is, the ten Lords of Appeal in Ordinary, the nine Lords of Appeal and the benches of the divisions of the High Court – revealed that of the sixty-nine Judges seventy-six per cent went to major public schools and the same percentage went to Oxford and Cambridge. Subsequent surveys have confirmed that very little has changed. They show that the higher up the judicial hierarchy more members are found to have attended public schools, mainly Winchester, Eton and Charterhouse, and more are found to have attended Oxford and Cambridge. A higher proportion gave their recreation as hunting, fishing, shooting, yachting and golf.

This elitist position has developed over the centuries. Indeed, during the nineteenth century patronage was openly practised in all levels of the judiciary and it continued until the 1930s when, because of the vocal militancy of a strong working-class movement, the judiciary loudly proclaimed it was independent and above politics. Appointments of an open political nature became rarer, but the practice continues in a more clandestine manner. Officially the reasons for the selection of a particular judge are never given, and the most said is that political considerations play no part in the appointment of judges.

How independent are judges and their trials? Once in office they have the protection of the various Acts that flowed from the Act of Settlement of 1700 and they cannot be removed from office for the decisions they make. But judges themselves have varying backgrounds and attitudes and they have varying perceptions of their role. It is well recognized that these factors alone influence their opinions and decisions. When these factors interact with the security they enjoy and their remote elevation, they are liable to acquire slanted views on certain aspects of life. Indeed, the Royal Commission on Assize and Quarter Sessions of 1966/9 advocated the movement of judges between civil and criminal courts and commented '. . . if they do occasionally develop idiosyncrasies as a result of the exalted seclusion in which they live, then their foibles move with them and do not become a source of irritation or amusement to any one section of the community'. It is well known in the legal profession that judges develop characteristic attitudes to certain offences and to their punishment, some being known as severe on particular offences while others are benevolent. Solicitors can often predict the outcome of a case from which particular judge is presiding at the court. Similarly it is not difficult for court support staff to influence the outcome of a case by arranging for it to be heard when a particular judge is sitting, or alternatively arranging for a particular judge to sit when the case has been set down for hearing, although it would be extremely difficult to prove that it has been done. The person arranging the court would receive a general suggestion from his superior that a certain course of action would avoid inconvenience for the department and may be in the interests of the more senior officers who are responsible for career prospects of the junior staff. The source of the suggestion might be traced through the support staff hierarchy to their political masters in the Lord Chancellor's Department and, as those 'deemed' to be civil servants are subject to the Official Secrets Act, no one outside the department would be likely to hear of the matter. If such a manipulation was suspected, without sufficient evidence to establish the means by which it was carried out, both the public and Parliament would be reluctant to voice the suspicion because of the sensitivity which exists concerning the alleged independence of the judiciary.

Indeed, decisions of a highly controversial nature have been supported by all political parties, and Parliament has not granted the Parliamentary Commissioner power to inquire into any matters that are subject to the decisions of the court.

So the judiciary may not be as independent as the Queen's Bench Masters would have us believe. To enable it to be so, as a first step, the Lord Chancellor's position would have to be made non-political, and the present Lord Chancellor's Department, or at least that part of it concerned with the courts and their operation, would have to be removed from the executive and operated as an entirely independent body. Although this would grant the entire judiciary independence, unfortunately it would not be accountable for its actions or decisions to any authority.

Whatever role a judge is considered to fulfil, whether it is merely to declare the law literally or whether it is to interpret it, he has to exercise a choice between alternative solutions all of which may be legally justified. His eventual decisions constitute precedents until they are overruled, and this gives rise to the thesis that judges make the law. The thesis has not been convincingly challenged. Careful investigations undertaken by social scientists have shown that unconscious political bias has permeated decisions of the courts, most often those concerning industrial relations or other politically sensitive matters on which strong feelings exist.

In the circumstances there appears to be no justification in a democracy for judges to claim an independence from all authority in the sense that they cannot be dismissed by anyone, even if the community disapproves of the policy choices a particular judge is making for it. However, because of the awe in which the judiciary is held, no parliamentary party or legal organization, and not even the public, has challenged the method by which judges are appointed, although it is demonstrably undemocratic and fundamentally wrong for the nation to have as lawmakers judges who are appointed on the recommendations of the Prime Minister or the Lord Chancellor (a member of the executive) and are thereafter independent and outside the control of any authority. It seems obvious that persons making the law on important moral and political issues should be elected by and accountable to the public and should be capable of being removed by the community after a set term of office; as the parliamentary parties reflect the opposing political philosophies of the day, they should nominate those they favour to act as judges and leave their appointment to a full-blooded contested national election. The Lord Chancellor could remain head of the judiciary and President of Chancery Division but would not be a Member of Parliament. The entire support staff of all the courts throughout the land, from the Magistrates' Courts and the County Courts to the Highest Appeal Court of the Law Lords, would be an independent and autonomous body, free from any possible influence from the executive and free from the last vestiges of the subtle system of political patronage within the judiciary.

This would place the feet of judges firmly on the ground and bring to them the realization that their position depends on the community they serve and that they would have to keep abreast of current social trends and movements in public opinion. Above all, while it would make the entire legal system independent, it would make the judges accountable to the community.

It has been suggested that the election of the judicature is against the constitution, which has always protected the independence of judges and kept them immune from external pressure. This may well be so, but there are no valid reasons for it to continue to be so. While the judges should be kept immune from bribery, and independent in that they should not be biased against one party to an action, they should not be immune from pressure to conform to the views of the community they serve. The legal profession argues that modern-day judges are not lawmakers. They claim that a judge's role is to interpret general rules in the light of specific cases. It is for them to apply the *litera legis* of the statute, in that they must be guided by the precise words used and unless there are clear indications in the statute that the words are employed in a special or technical sense, they must interpret them in the ordinary or dictionary sense. Where there are doubts as to the meaning, the judge must use the rules of interpretation that have grown up over time. For instance, if two clauses of a statute are inconsistent the later prevails and he must use the Ejusdem Generis rule of interpretation so that general terms must be restricted in their operation to the specific matters in the provisions of the statute.

This argument by the legal profession follows the traditional view, put forward by Blackstone many years ago in his *Commentaries*, that English judges merely declare and do not make the law. According to this view judges are limitless depositories of legal knowledge, being oracles who declare an eternal and immutable law. It is not for them to pronounce a deviation from the existing interpretation of the law but to maintain and expand existing interpretations. The lawyers assume that the legal answer to virtually any problem may be discovered by the appropriate use of legal knowledge, logic and analogies and that there is consequently a predictability of outcome in most legal issues. But this cannot be so, because a predictable law cannot be maintained in a changing progressive society. Every change in the law, however trivial, would have to come from Parliament and the judicial system would grind to a halt before Parliament could deal with the trivia. Indeed, parliamentary time for statutory intervention does not come about when the need for change is generally recognized but when the demand for it has become so overwhelming that action is forced upon the politicians. Furthermore, if judges operated like predictable machines, as indirectly suggested by some of the legal profession, it would be difficult to understand why they should be assumed to be of high intellectual calibre and why they are paid large salaries. If judgments were mechanical the necessity for Appeal Courts and trained lawyers could be questioned.

Of course the junior judges in the Crown Courts and the County Courts have little opportunity to participate in lawmaking, and to that extent the legal profession may well be right, but further up the judicial hierarchy, social and political views become steadily more important. In the Court of Appeal the judges are primarily concerned to see that the judge in the first instance applied the correct doctrine correctly. They are also to some extent concerned with the proper interpretation of fact. But to a greater extent than at the trial, the Court of Appeal is concerned to develop doctrines by deciding whether some particular principle should embrace the fact situation with which they are faced; or alternatively they are required to decide within which of two or more competing legal principles the case situation falls. This creative role becomes of far greater importance in the final Court of Appeal – the House of Lords. Although the judges there operate within the framework of legal principles, they are enabled to perform an essentially creative function by extending or failing to extend some particular legal doctrine or by interpreting a particular statute or section of an Act in a general or specific manner. Since 1966 the House of Lords has openly claimed the right to overrule a principle established in an earlier decision. Such changes may be different both in degree and in type from those brought about by Acts of Parliament, but many decisions by the House of Lords sitting as a judicial body do make important changes in the law. In 1966 Lord Radcliffe brought the matter into the open when he stated that '. . . there was never a more sterile controversy than that upon the question whether a judge makes law. Of course he does. How can he help it? . . . Judicial law is always a reinterpretation of principles in the light of new combinations of fact . . . Judges do not reverse principles once well established, but they do modify them, extend them, restrict them and even deny their application to the combination in hand.'

Professor Chapman stated in 1962 that one of the most striking features of the British legal system in European eyes is the arrogant presumption of High Court judges that in some way they, rather than Parliament, are the ultimate interpreters of public morality and the ultimate guardians of the public good. The legal profession, and particularly the judges, normally conceal the creative aspect of their work. In their judgments in court they do this by giving the appearance of applying precedent. Their tendency to conceal or reluctance to articulate the true nature of judicial decision-making has been one of the major factors adversely influencing the development of the modern legal system. As the judiciary insists that it has no concern with policy issues, the community cannot have confidence in it when it has to handle disputes that indirectly involve complex policy issues. Indeed, if the argument of the legal profession is soundly based, judges are unable to handle complicated commercial matters or labour problems because they involve policy issues, and consequently they are unable to serve the community in a section of law that is becoming increasingly important. This supports the contention that judges should be elected by the community, and those of them who feel that they are not accountable to the community and refuse to stand for election should be replaced.

The whole legal profession raises its hands in horror at such a suggestion and points to the politically motivated elected judges of the

United States of America and to the limitations that Congress can impose upon the jurisdiction of the American Supreme Court under section 2 of Article III of the Constitution of the United States. However, it is not suggested that the American example of the election of judges could or should be introduced into England and Wales. Indeed it is not only a system that should be particularly avoided, but one that should be reversed in Britain.

The deeply entrenched American conception of the sanctity of law derives from Europe and particularly England, and the Declaration of Independence and the American Constitution are coloured with the notion of the Rule of Law. It was, of course, natural for colonists when declaring independence either to reframe their colonial charters or to adopt new constitutions with the colonial charters in mind, but the fact that they felt compelled to have constitutions, and written ones, strongly implied that they believed in a law superior to executive decrees. A number of former colonies adopted a legal system similar to the British system, but in the case of America, because of its federal infrastructure, its legal system had to differ from that of England. Its courts were accordingly structured into federal courts and state courts and the federal courts are divided into two major categories. Firstly, there are the legislative courts, created by Congress with the power granted to it by the Constitution. These deal with matters that require a specialized form, such as the court of claims, the court of customs and patent appeals, the customs courts, the tax courts and the courts of military appeals. The judges in those courts are appointed by the President with Senate confirmation only for a set term and their decisions are reviewable by one of the second category of courts – the constitutional courts, comprising the District Court, the Courts of appeal and above all the United States Supreme Court. The Supreme Court has appellate jurisdiction over cases in the lower federal courts and the decisions of the highest courts in the individual states (see page 163). Furthermore, it has wide discretion on what it will in fact hear. The judges of the constitutional courts are appointed by the President, with Senate confirmation, and, subject to good behaviour and provided they are not impeached, their positions cannot be vacated during their lifetime, nor their salaries reduced during their continuance of office.

The judges in the federal system become involved in the politics of the nation and they are usually men who have had active political careers in their own states. Many federal judges have had state legislative experience and have used their state political connections to move into the federal judicial service, usually through the patronage system. Political considerations obviously play a substantial part in the process of federal judges. The American Constitution does not say how large the 'one Supreme Court' should be, nor does it specify the limits of its appellate jurisdiction. As the Constitution leaves these matters for Congress to decide, Congress has a good deal to say about the scope of judicial activity and the appointment of judges. Indeed, Congress is very much aware of the political nature of the court system, as evidenced by the reluctance of the Congress controlled by Democrats during the Eisenhower Administration to provide for much needed judges in the federal system. Congress waited until a Democrat, John F. Kennedy, occupied the White House before creating new judges, so that they could be filled by deserving Democrats rather than Republicans appointed by Eisenhower.

In most states the judges are elected to the state courts and they must by the nature of the case get into the political wars. Furthermore, they are without question an integral part of the political process. Their political role is not a matter of choice but of function. Like legislators and Presidents, they represent sets of values that they themselves must accommodate. They must make choices and are subject to the stresses and strains of society just as anyone else is. Any American judge attempting to separate himself from the political arena would be doomed to failure. But despite the criticisms that have been raised against the American legal system, it is apparent in today's society that the United States Supreme Court is the nation's exemplar and disseminator of democratic values. The country has become accustomed to look to the courts for guide-lines, standards and ideals; goals to which communal action ought to strive because the court stands resolute in its constitutional position as defender of the right, as it sees the right.

There is a degree of similarity in the appointment and in the security of tenure of the United States Senior Constitutional judges and the British High Court judges. In Britain, the Lords of Appeal in Ordinary, the Lord Justices of Appeal, the Lord Chief Justice, the Master of the Rolls and the President of the Family Division are appointed on the recommendation of the Prime Minister. The Lord Chancellor (a member of the executive) recommends the appointment of other judges. The one major difference between the appointment of senior judges in Britain and in the United States is that the appointment of judges in America must be confirmed by Congress. This power of Congress together with its not inconsequential interest in and direction of the Supreme Court hardly grants the appellate courts independence, but it is at this level that judicial law is made and that independence is essential for the impartial operation of the Rule of Law.

It is at this level also that it is suggested that the British judges should be elected to office for a set term of years. They would then be responsible for the entire work carried out at present by the Lord Chancellor's Department. They alone would be responsible for the appointment of the puisne judges (judges of the High Court of inferior rank) and all circuit judges throughout the country. Such appointments would be for life, subject only to removal for incompetence or incompatible behaviour decided by a majority of elected judges. To ensure that only experienced persons could be appointed to the upper echelons of the judiciary, the candidates for election, other than those already holding an elected office within the judiciary, should be puisne judges nominated by the parliamentary parties, or, in exceptional cases, circuit judges.

This would focus the senior judge's attention on the expectations of the community, trends in society and what society required of them in changing circumstances. If they ignored them by erroneously considering that they alone were guardians of public morals or that they knew what was best for society, they could be removed at the next election without the stigma of dismissal. They could once again become puisne judges, who are not lawmakers but whose decisions are subject to a higher court. If their services continued to be unsatisfactory they could be removed by the elected judges. Above all, this would ensure that the lawmaking judges were accountable to the community for the decisions they make on its behalf.

7

JURIES

Since twelve honest men have decided the cause,
And were judges of fact, tho' not judges of laws.

WILLIAM PULTENEY, EARL OF BATH, *The Honest Jury* (1731)

The origins of the jury system cannot be precisely determined. Early traces of a jury system are to be found in the oath helpers who existed in the times of the Anglo-Saxons, and it is on record that in 866-71 the laws of Ethelred provided that twelve freeholders of each 'hundred' should swear not to accuse an innocent person or to conceal a guilty one; but apart from the bare factual references, the precise origin of the Anglo-Saxon system is uncertain. Indeed, the Danes brought with them a system of settling land disputes by the sworn verdict of a group of local people.

It was at the Assize of Clarendon in 1166 that Henry II established a definite form of jury. It was a grand jury or a jury of presentment – that is its main task was to bring local criminals before the king's justices for trial. The notion behind the grand jury was that it constituted a representative body which could accuse persons too powerful for a single person to confront, and it was therefore an early law-enforcement agency. Henry II also introduced petty juries into royal courts. They were a body of neighbours summoned by a public officer to answer questions on oath. It was a royal administrative device, whereby representatives of the locality were required to offer information to the Crown regarding the customs, traditions and public life of the locality. Such information might include administrative, financial or judicial matters and usually these were concerned with the maintenance of bridges, rights of way and all community facilities. However, it was in its judicial capacity that the facts of the case were determined. It was a convenient and more acceptable method for deciding the issue between litigants than medieval methods such as trial by battle and trial by ordeal.

The jury trial became not only accepted but highly valued as a constitutional procedure in common law. Juries not only provided information for the king's judges and found the facts of a case, but they acted as intermediaries between the accused and the judges and protected the judges from the direct wrath of the populace when unpopular decisions were made. No explanations can be found why judges came to permit a body, which was instituted for the purpose of furnishing them with information and facts, to take a far more prominent position in legal trials and become not the suppliers of information or facts but the judges of the truth of the facts given in evidence during the trial. For centuries the guilt or innocence of the accused depended on what the jury knew or what the jury said it knew. The court received no other evidence and the jury not only provided the evidence of facts and customs but also used their own knowledge of the circumstances of the case, the accused and the offence. Statutes as far back as King Henry V I I were concerned with jurors and particularly what was to be done about Welsh jurors who gave 'untrue verdict against the King'.

In the seventeenth century the judges realized that the outcome of legal matters had been taken out of their hands, and they began to assume a large measure of control over verdicts. Thereafter, juries were to decide the facts given in evidence, and if they wished to use their own knowledge of the case they would have to appear in the proceedings as witnesses. In addition the judges assumed immense power over the jury by appropriating the extremes of either end of a factual dispute by maintaining that they were the sole arbiters of the law and that whether there was sufficient evidence to sustain a proposition of fact was a question of law. Further, whether a proposition was so overwhelmingly sustained that its rejection would be perverse was also a matter of law.

Consequently, they gave directions to the juries on matters interpreted as matters of law, and jurors who failed to follow those directions were considered disobedient and were punished by fines or imprisonment. Judges tried many ways to get out of the juries the verdicts they wanted. They bullied, browbeat, scolded and cajoled, shutting up juries without meat, drink, fire or candle until they agreed.

A formidable conflict between judge and jury took place in 1670, when the jury that had acquitted William Penn was imprisoned. Later in that year Chief Justice Vaughan released the jury under a writ of Habeas Corpus. Nevertheless, the affronted judge was able to set aside the verdict, which he deemed to be contrary to the law. He could then, in theory at least, continue to order new trials until he found a jury that would give the verdict he wanted. As a result of this unsatisfactory state of affairs, the rule against double jeopardy became firmly rooted in law; it stated that no verdict whereby the defendant was acquitted could be set aside, and thereafter no judge could shake the rule, although there was great argument among the judges concerning it. Some were of the opinion that it would lead to anarchy if juries rejected law to proclaim their verdicts.

In 1784 Lord Chief Justice Mansfield said that a judge could tell the jury how to do right, but they had it 'within their power to do wrong'. That, however, was a matter entirely between God and their consciences. In those words he recognized the sovereignty of the jury. Consciously or unconsciously, he was using the formula which Bracton had applied four centuries earlier to the king: 'The king is bound to obey the law, though if he breach it, his punishment must be left to God.'

The judges continued in their reluctance to surrender their influence over the outcome of the cases they dealt with. The situation came to a head in the celebrated trial of the Dean of St Asaph for seditious libel. Without going into the details of the case, it was apparent that the Dean received a pamphlet which he did not read but which was forwarded for translation and printing in Welsh. It was clear to the judges that it would be difficult to secure a jury that would return a verdict of guilty, notwithstanding a direction by the judge that the publication was libellous. They therefore resorted to a technical, though devious, device to obtain the verdict they desired. They realized that if the jury acquitted it would mean 'Not Guilty' both in law and fact. Although the jury takes the law from the judge, there are not two separate issues, one of law and one of fact, demanding two separate decisions. Accordingly, the accused cannot be made to plead separately to issues of law and issues of fact, and a general plea blends fact and law together. On an acquittal there was nothing that could be done about it, but this could, perhaps, be avoided by asking the jury for a special verdict – one finding certain facts proved or otherwise but leaving the law to the judge. This was a procedure often used but intended for cases where there was a difficult question of law which the judge could not be expected to solve on the spot. It was successful, and judges endeavoured to establish this procedure in ordinary criminal cases. Juries, however, became aware of the ruse and refused a special verdict whenever they suspected a scheme on the part of the judge. Nevertheless, judges continued to exploit the peculiarities of the procedure in libel cases to obtain the result they required.

In the case of libel the procedure required that the whole libel should be set out on record. In this way the question of law was separated from fact. So the juries were directed on proof of publication to find the accused 'Guilty', but the jury were assured that, if they did so, they were finding him 'Guilty' only on the record and if the record disclosed no libel, the accused would be freed on a motion to arrest judgment. This procedure was adopted by judges in all libel cases until Fox's Libel Act 1792 reversed the judicial position by declaring that, in any trial or information of libel, the jury might give a general verdict of guilty or not guilty on the whole matter. The Act also contained the proviso that, in trials for criminal libel, the judge might give 'his opinions and directions to the jury in the matter in issue . . . in like manner as in other criminal cases'.

This narrow concept of fact has been continually subject to argument, but the power of the jury has prevailed despite the wishes of the judges over the centuries. Blackstone wrote: 'Trial by jury ever has been and I trust ever will be looked upon as the glory of English law; it is the most transcendent privilege which any subject can enjoy or wish for, that he cannot be affected either in his property, his liberty, or his person, but by the unanimous consent of twelve of his neighbours and equals.' Such sentiments remain strong, and the source of the jury's power lay, and still lies, in a tradition which by the eighteenth century had gone on for so long as to have developed into a constitutional principle. For five hundred years or more, a person charged with a crime had had the right to 'put himself on his country' by electing to be tried by a jury of his peers. If he was found not guilty, it was as if he had survived trial by ordeal, which trial by jury had replaced. The unanimous verdict of a jury was treated almost as a sign from heaven.

Over the centuries there was great opposition to the creation of new tribunals, such as courts composed of Justices of the Peace or courts of conscience, in which jury trial was not available. Pressure was exerted to introduce jury trials in all courts, and in the mid nineteenth century provision was made for them not only in the Chancery Courts but even in the County Courts. Paradoxically, it was at about the same time that there was an increasing recognition of the fact that jury trial was not appropriate in all cases, particularly in minor cases, and that summary proceedings would be more convenient.

History has shown that there have been three kinds of juries, which differed in constitution and purpose. Firstly there was the grand jury, in origin the earliest. The sheriff was required to return to every sessions and to every assize twenty-four good and lawful men of the county 'to inquire, present, do and execute all those things . . . which should be commanded of them'. They were to be freeholders and in Blackstone's view they were 'usually gentlemen of the best figure in the county'. At least twelve of them were selected and the judge upon the bench instructed them on the articles of their inquiry and, typically, his charge to the grand jury would be to survey the state of crime in the area and offer his own thoughts on it.

The grand jury then withdrew to sit and to receive indictments which were preferred to them in the name of the king, but at the suit of any private prosecutor. Since the task of the grand jury was merely to determine whether there was sufficient cause to call on the party charged to answer the accusations, it heard only the prosecution's evidence. Its duties were assumed by the Magistrates' Courts on indictments and the grand jury was abolished in 1933.

Another extinct type of jury is the special jury. Either plaintiff or defendant could choose to have their case heard not before a judge and common jury but before a judge and special jury consisting of persons who, in addition to possessing the ordinary qualification of interest in land, were of a certain station in society – persons of high degree, bankers or merchants. According to Blackstone, such juries had been introduced when the causes in the cases were of too great a nicety for discussion by ordinary freeholders or when the sheriff was suspected of partiality. Lord Mansfield made use of such juries when he was developing the principles of commercial law. They were objected to as far back as the end of the eighteenth century, particularly in criminal cases, and by 1824 they were subject to general criticism because of the lack of intelligence, education and social standing of very many special jurymen. By the early years of the twentieth century the use of the special jury in criminal cases had almost died out, but their use continued in personal injury cases because of the belief that people of high status were likely to think in larger terms when it came to assessing damages. However, in 1913 a Home Office Committee became concerned with the gradual widening of the qualification for membership of a special jury and it was eventually abolished in 1949.

The ordinary or common jury survives to this day. In the early days the juries at the Assize Courts tended to be composed of the gentry, for the visit of the Assize judge rivalled the fair and pageant as an event in the social calendar. The juries of the Quarter Sessions tended to be far less socially exalted. The chief qualification of a juror was that he must hold one of a number of interests in land, a qualification which was consolidated in the Juries Act of 1825 and was not unduly criticized by the Home Office Committee sitting as late as 1913.

During the fourteenth century the number of jurors was fixed at twelve. The jurors were called to serve by officials drawing successively out of a box the names of those jurors on the panel previously selected by qualification. The first twelve persons called and present were sworn as the jury, unless some form of objection or excuse was brought forward. Such challenge could be made on the grounds of partiality on the part either of the sheriff who had drawn up the panel of jurors or the individual jurors themselves.

Although the jury system has had a chequered history, in a democracy law is made by the will of the people and obedience is given not from fear but from goodwill. The jury is the means by which people play a direct role in the application of the law. The interrelationship between the judge and the jury makes for a verdict not demagogic and ensures that the law is applied in a way that is not an affront to the conscience of the common man. It has already been pointed out that in those courts in which there was trial by jury, torture has played no part in obtaining confessions, while it has been evident in courts without juries.

Nowadays all judges accept trial by jury as part of the established order of things, but for some necessity plays a greater part in their acceptance than more elevated reasons. Even today the accused who is acquitted by the jury in a criminal case cannot be retried for the offence in question even if the judge considers the acquittal to be unreasonable. In cases in which the jury cannot arrive at a unanimous verdict and cannot even agree a verdict with a ten to two majority, a retrial must be held. If a second jury cannot agree a verdict at the retrial, the charges are usually dropped.

The position is rather different in civil cases. If it is felt that the jury has gone beyond the judicial bounds of reasonableness the appellate judges are not as powerless as they are in criminal cases. They do not have to accept the situation, and can set aside the verdict and order a new trial.

The selection of jurors is now laid down in the Juries Act 1974. All persons between the ages of 18 years and 65 years whose names are on the electoral register are liable for jury service, though there is a long list of exemptions including lawyers, clergymen, police officers, prison officers, members of Parliament, and military and naval personnel. The electoral register is marked accordingly and it is usual for about twenty of those names marked to be selected for the panel of jury members, of whom twelve are finally called and sworn in for jury service at a particular trial.

The officers of the Crown Court have available for each defendant a list of potential jurors (the jury panel) with their names and addresses. The accused, or his or her solicitor, can obtain copies of the lists when they consider it appropriate to do so. Although such lists formerly included the occupation of the juror, this requirement was removed by an amendment introduced by the Lord Chancellor. Whether by design or not this makes the procedure for challenging a juror more difficult. Indeed, a complete literature concerning the desirable constitution of juries in certain classes of crime has developed among lawyers. Among the imaginable categories of jurors on rape cases were those, for example, who were of the opinion that women were less likely to acquit a man charged with rape because they could identify themselves with the alleged victim. Defending lawyers also attempted to keep professional or intelligent people off juries involving complicated fraud in the hope that the remaining jurors would not be able to understand the financial convolutions of involved fraudulent business transactions or fraudulent trading by company directors. From the law-enforcement officer's view, it is extremely difficult to attempt to explain to a jury comprising the butcher, the baker and candlestick-maker the intricacies of the modern business world. They cannot assimilate documents or meaningfully read trading accounts and balance sheets. Consequently, it is virtually impossible to provide them with any idea of the position without preparing diagrams of decreasing assets and increasing liabilities etc. over a given period. However, diagrams, although helpful in certain cases, cannot always show a true picture, and if any manipulations cannot be explained to the jury there must be reasonable doubt as to the accused's guilt. It must then in all conscience acquit the accused. There is therefore a strong case for the reintroduction of the special jury.

For a long time the defendant could challenge up to seven members of the jury (presumably half the jury plus one), but by the Criminal Justice Act 1977 the number that could be challenged with no reason given was reduced to three. The Criminal Justice Bill (1986) proposes the complete abolition of the defence right to challenge without cause, but objections to jurors may be made if reasonable cause is given.

After the challenges have been dealt with, each member of the jury is sworn, and thereafter they have certain rights as jurors, though these are very rarely, if ever, pointed out to them. Firstly, a juror has the right to ask the judge or witnesses questions. When questions are asked the jury usually addresses them to the judge, because they may not be permitted under the laws of evidence. If they *are* permitted, the judge may then put the question to a witness on behalf of the jury. However, this procedure does not prejudice the juror's right to address a question to a witness. The second important right is that the jury has the power to stop a trial at the end of the prosecution's case. Again judges do not normally inform the jury of this right and counsel for the defence is not allowed to do so. In addition the jury has the right to inform the judge at any stage of the trial that they wish to discuss the case so far and ask leave to retire to the jury room, but few jurors are aware of the fact and it is a most infrequent occurrence.

The jury is, then, twelve people chosen from the electoral register at random, thrown together for the first time in the awe-inspiring atmosphere of the Law Courts, required to submit to an oath and then to sit in two rows at the side of the courtroom without the opportunity of being aware of the nature of the case before them, without being fully informed of their rights, and most importantly without the opportunity at that stage of nominating or appointing a spokesperson. At the end of the trial the jury has to consider its verdict, and for that purpose the members usually leave for a retiring room, with the instructions given by the judge that they must elect a foreperson. The election is usually by a show of hands, by general acclamation or in some instances by secret ballot. This seems to put the cart before the horse — the election of a foreperson should take place immediately the jury has been sworn in to enable him or her to speak for the jury in addressing questions and requests to the judge and in questioning witnesses.

Until recent years, a jury had to be unanimous in finding a verdict. If that could not be achieved, a retrial had to be held. It is the practice that when a second jury cannot agree, the charges are dropped — there is no third trial. However, there came a point when in a number of important cases successive juries failed to agree on a verdict and the wrongdoer escaped punishment, not because he was innocent but because the juries could not agree. It was at least suspected that in certain major criminal trials friends of the defendant were bribing or threatening a juror into refusing a verdict to convict in both the first and the second trial, enabling the accused to go free. To overcome this problem the Criminal Justice Act 1967 introduced verdicts whereby a majority of ten to two jurors could be accepted. It would then require three jurors to be bullied, bribed or threatened, in each trial, into voting not guilty to influence the verdict. This may or may not have been successful in achieving its object, but it is surprising how often juries still fail to arrive at a decision on a ten to two basis.

Although jurors are not sworn to secrecy and their oath does not contain any such commitment, officially no one knows what goes on in the jury room. A notice in the room informs them that as jurors they are not supposed to tell what happens there and a breach of those regulations can be dealt with by the court as contempt under the Contempt of Court Act 1981. Nevertheless, from a limited survey of jurors it seems that they have been completely perplexed by court procedures, though most have found the experience enjoyable except when they could identify themselves with the accused. They were more certain in their decision when the nature of the crime was alien to them, but otherwise they have introduced humanity into harsh laws. This was confirmed by evidence given to a Home Office Select Committee that juries showed reluctance to convict motorists of manslaughter because they felt the penalties for manslaughter were too severe on the evidence produced. They preferred a verdict of dangerous driving. The Committee accepted the view that a judge should agree to a jury introducing not only a verdict of dangerous driving in cases of manslaughter, but also a verdict of driving without due care and attention.

Although most jurors accept the position in which they find themselves without complaint, a great deal of criticism of the system seems to have some justification. One juror in the Inner London Crown Court, writing in a Sunday newspaper, stated: 'We were empanelled for a fortnight, which in my case overran by some way. For long periods of the time many of us were kept hanging around, in rooms or corridors, either waiting to be called, or, if we had been called, waiting outside court to be summoned inside by jury selection. Jury service seemed rather like being in a conscript army at the start of war – hours, even days, of sitting around, punctuated by unexplained roll calls, shipment to a distant quarter to continue waiting, above all nothing explained or apologized for. It was not unusual for a juror to spend two and a half days doing nothing.'

This particular juror sat in five cases during his service. In the first the accused was charged with assaulting his wife and two police officers. He was found guilty on one charge and ordered to pay £20 compensation to the police officer. In the second case the defendant was charged with stealing a 'pass' worth £2.80 and found not guilty. In the third case a young man was accused of being in possession of an offensive weapon – a small kitchen knife. He was found guilty and remanded for reports. In the fourth case a young lad was accused of stealing petrol worth £5 from a self-service station and driving while disqualified. He was found not guilty. The last case involved a casual worker who was accused of stealing two bottles of wine and some scraps of food from his employers. The wine, incidentally, was recovered by the employers. The defendant was found guilty and fined £120 and £100 costs. Many other jurors have complained about the trivial cases that they have had to deal with.

On the information provided by this juror and others, it seems to be a dreadful waste of time and public money to require twelve jurors in addition to a highly paid judge, not to mention the court support staff, to attend and deal with such cases. As it now costs more than £1,000 a day to try a case before a jury, for trivial matters it seems to be an expensive exercise, fruitless for everyone except the lawyers, who receive a high proportion of the cost. Of course, in virtually all the minor instances brought before the court the defendants have elected to put their case to a jury in the hope that they would stand a better chance with twelve ordinary citizens than with three Justices of the Peace or a stipendiary magistrate. However, it is hardly credible that all those defendants came to elect for trial before a jury without being recommended to do so by their lawyers. It also seems significant that they were all issued legal aid certificates.

It may be that lawyers feel that the modern jury protects the accused not from torture or excessive pressure but for some reason provides the accused with a better chance of acquittal than he or she would have with a magistrate. Indeed, the fact that twelve men (more recently men and women) have had to consider the veracity of the evidence before them and decide whether or not the accused has done those things for which he has been charged gives confidence to the accused and to the community that a fair and usually true verdict has been arrived at. However, that confidence is based on the assumption that the jury is capable of understanding the evidence before them. If there is any reasonable doubt in the jurors' minds concerning the innocence or guilt of the accused, the latter, whether guilty or not, must be discharged. But what constitutes 'reasonable doubt' cannot be clearly laid down for the jury's guidance. Obviously, if the jury does not understand the evidence, there must be doubt in the juror's mind. The difficulties encountered in complex fraud cases have already been referred to, but a more important source of difficulty is encountered which may become more acute as our technical knowledge progresses. The computerization of financial institutions has rendered them liable to computer frauds. The technical methods of coding into computer data banks is difficult to explain even to professional men if they are unacquainted with complex programming techniques. How then can a randomly selected jury have anything but doubt concerning the innocence or guilt of a person charged on such evidence? If the jury has to rely upon the directions of the judge on questions of fact, or upon the evidence and opinions of experts without understanding what they are saying, the whole purpose of having a jury is defeated. On 10 January 1986, the Fraud Trials Committee under Lord Roskill recommended the abolition of jury trials in complex fraud cases and the setting-up of Fraud Trials Tribunals made up of a judge sitting with two specially qualified laymen. Fierce opposition to the proposals were made by the Criminal Bar Association, the Criminal Law Committee of the Law Society and the civil liberties groups.

If this alone is not sufficient reason for the provision of specialist juries there is also the fact that, under random selection, persons who have been charged on previous occasions and convicted of criminal offences have an equal chance with others of being selected to serve on a jury, and even those previously convicted of an offence similar to the one being tried are not excluded. Such jurors are likely to identify themselves with the accused, and as more and more people are brought before the courts or fined in their absence in respect of minor motoring offences, the more likely there are to be on a jury those not prepared to return a guilty verdict. The modern common jury system thus weighs heavily in favour of the accused.

Finally, two other forms of jury totally unconnected with criminal proceedings must be mentioned. At certain inquests at Coroners' Courts held in England, Wales and Northern Ireland, and at fatal accident inquiries in Scotland, a jury is required to consider and return a verdict on the cause and when and where the deceased person met his or her death. These juries consist of between seven and eleven jurors, and the Coroner may accept a majority verdict provided that the minority consists of not more than two. A jury is also required at an inquest held by a Coroner to consider whether gold or silver objects found in the ground are 'treasure trove' (hidden treasure of unknown ownership).

8

THE LEGAL PROFESSION

> He saw a lawyer killing a viper
> On a dunghill hard by his own stable;
> And the devil smiled, for it put him in mind
> Of Cain and his brother, Abel.

S. T. COLERIDGE and R. SOUTHEY, *The Devil's Thoughts* (1799)

An address given on 11 May 1974 by Gerald Sanctuary of the Professional and Public Relations office of the Law Society, as reported in the *New Law Journal* on 6 June 1974, contained the following passage: 'There is therefore much to be done if we are to be perceived by the public as we think we should be. It is comforting to know that we are reasonably well trusted, and indeed accepted as one of the essential professional services. Yet it is worrying, to say the least, that the extent of our real competence is not appreciated. Why is it worrying? *Because we have to live in an egalitarian society*' (my italics). He went on to say: 'The world in which we work is not static. We must adapt ourselves to rapidly changing times. The profession of law is not only useful, it is essential. If lawyers did not exist, it would be necessary to invent them.'

Nevertheless, the organization of the legal profession has remained unchanged for the last two hundred years. Indeed, as the quotation confirms, the attitude of lawyers to their profession has ensured that law has attracted into its ranks few outside the professional middle class.

English law has always allowed full liberty to the individual to conduct his own case in court, both in the initial and final stages of the proceedings, if he thinks fit to do so. But the right to represent a litigant legally is the exclusive monopoly of a barrister – a man or woman called to the Bar of one of the Inns of Court – or a solicitor – a member of the Law Society. This division of the legal profession in England has existed for at least six centuries – as both parts of it are found almost from the beginning of common law it is difficult to say which is the older. Subject to the right of every litigant to act on his or her own behalf, any person not a barrister or solicitor who attempts to act on behalf of another as a legal practitioner, in court or otherwise, whether or not with a view to gain, incurs serious penalties and cannot enforce any promise of remuneration for his services which may have been made to him. The roots of the division of the legal profession and this monopoly are steeped in history. Originally, the barrister appears to have been a casual bystander in the courts who volunteered advice to a litigant and, having acquired a taste for the practice, gradually obtained recognition by the court as suitable to be 'of counsel' with litigants. This detached position survives in a most remarkable way in the modern rules of law and grants barristers privileges unwarranted in a modern profession (this is dealt with in later chapters). Suffice it to say, at this stage, that no barrister can make a binding contract for fees, or sue to recover them, nor can they bind their clients by anything they say in court. On the other hand they cannot be sued for negligence in the conduct of their clients' cases in court however negligent they have been. This follows because any payments to barristers, from earliest times, were regarded as gratuities, not as the payment of fees, and theoretically the situation remains the same today. Barristers pretended that they did not concern themselves with payment for their services and had a convenient pocket at the back of their gowns into which the gratuities were to be placed. They continue in their pretence of distaste for payment and leave such matters to their clerk of chambers. The pockets in their gowns have become ornamental relics.

Although barristers owed their opportunity of audience in court to a recognition by the court, they developed their own professional bodies. For centuries the privilege of 'calling to the Bar' – the investiture of a person with the forensic honour of barrister at law – has been exercised by four wealthy and powerful bodies known as the Inns of Court – Lincoln's Inn, Gray's Inn and the Middle and Inner Temples. These bodies are entirely self-governing. They are administered by bodies of 'Benchers' or Seniors, who publish no account of their proceedings, and they are practically uncontrolled by any Act of Parliament. Much about their origin remains obscure. They were originally voluntary clubs or associations or pleaders in the king's court at Westminster, set up in the twelfth and thirteenth centuries to administer the royal jurisdiction and in particular the newly formed common law. The Templars owe their ecclesiastical connection to the fact that on the dissolution of the Crusading Order of the Knights Templars in the early fourteenth century, the two bodies of lawyers moved from their former hostels, somewhere in the neighbourhood of High Holborn, to the older abodes of the Knights with its ancient church on the banks of the Thames. For some time after their foundation, the members of the Inns of Court received their clients personally, often in their chambers or at some public rendezvous like St Paul's Cathedral, and advised them indiscriminately about their affairs as a whole, not confining themselves to appearances in court or formal consultations.

Side by side with the barristers there existed the profession of legal attorneys (now solicitors). As their name implies, they were originally agents of litigants and they can be traced as far back in legal history as barristers. The earliest lawsuits were judicial duels, in which early law did not allow the parties to be represented by agents unless exceptional circumstances existed or one of the litigants was a woman or child. As the primitive judicial combat gave way to the ordered and technical lawsuit sometimes involving long and wearisome journeys, the privilege of being represented by an agent was increasingly sought, and was granted by the authorities of various jurisdictions. Naturally, the courts in which the agents appeared were interested in their identity and character, and by the end of the fourteenth century the king's court of common law had adopted the practice of inscribing on its walls or records the names of certain persons recognized as agents for the parties in the proceedings before them. This practice gave attorneys a privileged and close profession and established them as officials of the court.

Until the Restoration, barristers and attorneys dwelt in the same precincts and were closely associated, but thereafter the barristers began to adopt an exclusive attitude towards both their lay clients and the attorneys, who withdrew from their societies. The consequence of this autocratic policy was important. It enhanced the social prestige of barristers and enabled them to mix with courtiers and statesmen on more or less equal terms, thus opening for them the road to public offices of the highest distinction. They became an elitist group and have remained so ever since. On the other hand, it threw the attorney and the lay client together in the outer world, and as far as legal work was concerned the barrister, in those early days, was very much at the mercy of the attorney, who in fact became the barrister's client. Above all, the initial stages of all legal business, and the complete handling of much of it, fell into the hands of the attorney, whose position rapidly improved until he became a fully independent practitioner not only in the county towns, where there was no barrister to rival him, but also in London. Nevertheless, the barristers retained the right to transact business with a lay client, though nowadays, unless they are retained by the Crown or large corporation, they rely entirely on solicitors for their business.

Today the principal body concerned with the profession of barrister at law is the Senate of the Inns of Court and the Bar (a body created in 1960 by agreement between the four Inns of Court and the Bar Council), established to speak with a single voice on all matters on which the parties agreed and to present a common policy. The government of the profession is primarily in the hands of the General Council of the Bar, but the prospective barrister must have, among other things, satisfactorily completed courses of study and practice and passed the examinations laid down by the Council of Legal Education since its establishment in 1852. The Senate has adopted the policy of graduate entry, and the candidate must obtain admittance as a student to one of the four Inns of Court and 'keep' twelve terms by dining in the Hall a specified number of days each term. On fulfilment of the requirements the candidate is entitled to present himself for 'call to the Bar' at the next call-night of his or her Inn. Notice of this intention is placed on the notice boards of all the Inns of Court, and it is open to anyone to inform the Benchers of a candidate's Inn of any circumstances alleged to disqualify the candidate from being called. If no charge is made and proved, the duly qualified candidate is called to the Bar by ancient ceremony at the close of dinner on call-night and is thenceforth entitled to exercise all the privileges and functions of a barrister, though he must serve a period of pupillage.

The fully qualified barrister does not cease to be a member of the Inn. In all matters of professional conduct and personal character the barrister's Inn of Court is still guardian of the profession. The Inns of Court have never been democratic institutions – they have always been ruled by the Benchers. Abel-Smith and Stevens (1968) described them as self-perpetuating oligarchies. They say: 'There are . . . strong pressures on each barrister to conform to the ethics and traditions of the bar. An Inn is a club with a membership much more tightly knit than is customarily to be found in clubs located in the vicinity of Pall Mall. The ceremonies, rules and patterns of behaviour of each Inn, which are so reminiscent of a traditional boys' public school, all help to impose social control, and incidentally to make even minor changes exceptionally difficult.'

The Treasurer of Gray's Inn reinforced those observations when he defended the 'keeping of term' in an article in *The Times*: 'The training to become a barrister is intended to include not merely the acquisition of a sound knowledge of the law but the attainment through mutual association and companionship of an honourable status and code of professional conduct which gives prestige to members of the bar of England.'

Within the profession of barrister at law there is a comparatively small group of senior members of the legal elite known as 'Queen's Counsel' enjoying certain additional privileges. As they wear silk gowns in court, as distinct from the 'stuff' worn generally, they are also known as 'silks'. They do not constitute a different order from their brethren at the Bar, but by custom they receive somewhat higher fees for their work than the juniors or ordinary barristers and they have a priority of audience in court. They occupy an anomalous position in that they are Crown officials who remain members of and subject to the authority of their Inns of Court. The Bar maintains that the advantages of a silk system are, firstly, that it provides a career structure within the Bar; secondly, that it provides a cadre of highly skilled men and women who are free to devote themselves to the more complex and difficult cases, and finally that it provides a pool of recognized talent and integrity from which judicial and other appointments can be made.

How do barristers become Queen's Counsels? The answer has always been by unashamed patronage. Barristers apply in December for the appointment of Queen's Counsel, giving full details of their careers and the names of their sponsoring judges. The Lord Chancellor, working with his Permanent Secretary, first decides how many vacancies there are and then considers the requirements of the different circuits, the specialist Bars and the criminal and common law Bars. The names of the applicants are then reduced to a short list. After discussions, the Lord Chancellor makes his final selection, which is forwarded to the Queen and gazetted on the first day of the Easter vacation. At no stage is there consultation with the Bar. No reason for refusal is ever given and there is no recourse for an unsuccessful applicant save to try again next year. Barristers who continue to be unsuccessful must eventually reconcile themselves to the fact that they are considered unsuitable and that the heights of the profession are out of their reach. The Report of the Bar Council's Special Committee into the Silk System (June 1970, para. 21) states: 'The basis of the disquiet over the present system is that taking Silk represents the taking of a professional step with principally economic consequences for the individual and it is not easily acceptable that the decision should be dictated by means of an act of patronage wholly despotic however benevolent.'

In evidence given by the Bar to the Royal Commission on Legal Services it was said: 'The law must be impartial, and practising lawyers must be uncommitted. Only the law can hold the balance between the interests of the individual and those of the state, which is increasingly intervening in human affairs. Lawyers therefore must be specially independent of the executive . . . without an independent legal profession the citizen may be unable to discover his legal rights or to assert or defend them.' This claim to independence appears to be contradicted by the subtle influence of the exercise of patronage. There is not only a serious risk but a strong possibility that, as there are many more applications for silk than are granted, juniors wishing to take silk are concerned, probably unconsciously, to act in the way that they think most likely to commend them to any person who may influence the decision on their appointment. Indeed, the executive can use the patronage system as an initial filter of barristers and prevent those whom they think unsuitable for their purposes from ever being eligible for high office.

The Bar Council has itself acknowledged that silk is occasionally given to someone generally regarded by colleagues as thoroughly unworthy of it; and rather more frequently, juniors held in high regard by the Bar are refused silk after repeated applications. This is

in direct opposition to the argument that the system provides a pool
of recognized talent from which judicial appointments can be made
and to the argument that it provides a cadre of highly skilled men
who are free to devote themselves to the more complex and difficult
cases.

Virtually all other professions manage to function successfully
without anything resembling the silk system and without its in-built
patronage and yet are able to provide their members with career
opportunities. The more skilled and experienced accountants are able
to increase their fees and, indeed, specialize. Surgical consultants do
not concern themselves with appendectomies but devote themselves
to more complex cases. But the highly skilled surgeons are as well
known within the medical profession as able barristers are known
within the legal profession.

The only persons other than barristers permitted to carry on a legal
practice are known as 'solicitors of the Supreme Court'. Historically,
they are a combination of several totally distinct professions, those of
attorneys of the common law court, solicitors of the Court of
Chancery, proctors of the old ecclesiastical courts and the scriveners,
who until the end of the eighteenth century were a kind of high-class
law stationers.

As we have seen, the oldest element of those professions and the
one which had the greatest influence in defining the position of this
branch of the legal profession was that of attorney of the common
law courts. 'Solicitors' in the strict sense of the word were never
agents, but appeared in connection with Equity proceedings towards
the end of the sixteenth century, to 'solicit' causes which were too
long in the chambers of the Masters in Chancery. By the beginning
of the seventeenth century, they came to be regarded as a profession
like the attorneys, and before the middle of that century the two
professions were virtually consolidated into one. After their with-
drawal from the Inns of Court, when barristers went their own way,
attorneys and solicitors resorted to what were then known as Inns of
Chancery, institutions which were perhaps more ancient than the
Inns of Court but which never attained anything like the wealth and
recognition of the latter. Indeed, they became extinct by the end of
the eighteenth century and were replaced as professional institutions

by the Law Society. Meanwhile, the scriveners as a distinct profession became moribund by the end of the eighteenth century, their business passing into the hands of solicitors. Finally, in 1857 the extinction of the matrimonial and probate jurisdiction of the Church courts, combined with the decay of their other functions, extinguished the proctors as a separate profession and most of them joined the ranks of solicitors. The whole of the legal profession, other than the Bar, had then become merged as solicitors.

In 1860 the Law Society introduced a preliminary examination aimed at excluding entrants who were not 'gentlemen'. By the 1870s the Society had established itself as an effective trade union as well as a powerful force for the social elevation of its members, who received the official designation of 'solicitors of the Supreme Court' by the Judicature Act 1873. The Law Society stands in much the same position *vis-à-vis* solicitors as do the Inns of Court *vis-à-vis* barristers, with one very important difference. The barristers' qualification for admission to the profession depends entirely on tradition and custom as expounded by each Inn of Court on its own authority. In the case of solicitors, such matters are expressly fixed by Acts of Parliament, which the Law Society has to administer, and by the provisions to which it is bound. The actual admission of a solicitor to practise is the function of the Master of the Rolls, who holds a high judicial position as well as being the custodian of the vast stores of legal and other records accumulated in the Record Office. Consequently, the Council of the Law Society has a much less free hand than the Inns of Court.

A proportion of barristers are foreigners, and colonial and commonwealth citizens are very well represented in the Inns of Court. However, foreigners cannot become officials of English courts of justice and cannot, therefore, become solicitors, although membership of the solicitors' branch of the legal profession is open to all British subjects who acquire the necessary qualifications. These include admission as a student on fulfilling the requirements of general education, the serving of articles of clerkship to a practising solicitor, the attendance at a centre of legal education and the passing of qualifying examinations conducted by the Law Society. The qualified person would then be authorized to undertake such kinds of legal business as are open to solicitors generally. However, a solicitor's right of audience in open court is limited for the most part to inferior courts, though they can appear on procedural matters in any court before the judge or Master in Chambers (sitting privately).

The preliminary conduct of litigation is mainly the province of the solicitor, and the preparation of documents dealing with countless non-litigious legal interests of the members of the public he shares with the barrister, but the solicitor has virtual monopoly of dealing direct with the public. At company board meetings involving a large amount of important financial, commercial and industrial business, the solicitor of the institution is nearly always present, to advise upon legal questions which crop up in the course of discussion. In delicate family matters involving reputation and property, solicitors are invariably consulted. To the middle classes he is almost a judge, the representative and the expounder of the law.

The division of the legal profession is a costly and inefficient anachronism, but the powerful, wealthy and influential Inns of Court have been able to defeat any attempted encroachment on its rights and privileges. They were able to persuade the 1979 Royal Commission on Legal Services that separate qualifications in the legal profession were in the 'public interest', and in their evidence to the Commission the Bar claimed that, although there were many areas in which the functions of solicitors and barristers overlap, most clients liked to be able to take all their legal problems to one local solicitor and few of them needed the services of a barrister. If they did need someone highly specialized, a barrister was available for the solicitor to consult. They went on to say that the division of function between barrister and solicitor is efficient and economic, the Bar providing a complete range of special expertise and experience which is available to each firm of solicitors, however small. They asserted that the independence of the Bar, and the economic service which it was able to provide because of its freedom to concentrate on its work without the need for a large administrative organization, would be lost in a fused profession. It was a fallacy, they maintained, to suggest that the division of the profession into two branches was wasteful of manpower. Wasteful to whom, one wonders.

People involved in litigation find themselves in a bewildering position. Their case may find itself passing through four or five hands on its way to trial. A solicitor is initially instructed and if the matter is to be dealt with in the High Court the solicitor contacts a barrister's clerk in the appropriate chambers. He passes the matter on to the barrister whom he considers most suitable in those chambers. An appointment is sometimes made for the litigant to provide background information to counsel and the litigant frequently has to travel considerable distances to keep that appointment, often to find that counsel has been detained in court on a case that has lasted longer than anticipated. The litigant wastes hours and possibly days. Eventually, having discussed the matter with counsel, who may be head or a senior in the chambers, the litigant may find that the barrister with whom he has discussed the problem, sometimes more than once, does not appear in their case. The matter is often re-routed through the clerk of the chambers to a less experienced barrister, who often has less than twenty-four hours to familiarize himself or herself with the matter. If a senior, who is likely to be a Queen's Counsel, does attend the hearing, the poor litigant may be faced with the cost of two barristers. Numerous other examples of waste and inefficiency could be quoted. Nevertheless, in a White Paper the government accepted the Royal Commission's recommendations that there should be no general extension of solicitors' right of audience despite its declared intention to shake up traditional boundaries between the professions, and it also accepted that there should be no fusion of the legal profession. However, the continuation of the *status quo* on this particular matter is hardly surprising. Of the members of the Cabinet at the time, the Prime Minister, Mrs Thatcher, the Foreign Secretary, Sir Geoffrey Howe, the Home Secretary, Leon Brittan, the Education Secretary, Sir Keith Joseph, and the Environment Secretary, Patrick Jenkin, were all barristers. Moreover, Lord Hailsham, the Lord Chancellor, and Sir Michael Havers, the Attorney General, both powerful in government circles and both barristers, were known to oppose fusion of the legal profession.

The Law Society argued for many years that litigants should be able to retain the advocate of their choice and not have to employ more lawyers than were absolutely necessary for their case. In March 1984, faced with government legislation to end the solicitors' monopoly of conveyancing, the Society pressed for removal of the barristers' monopoly of rights of audience in the higher courts. It argued that if the Prime Minister really wanted to be seen as head of a government that tackled monopolies in the professions, it could not ignore the Bar's monopoly, which excluded solicitors from appearing for clients in the higher courts. It claimed that solicitors should have equal rights of audience with barristers. Sir Arthur Power, secretary of the Bar Council, said that the Bar was 'particularly unimpressed' by the Law Society's reasons for seeking the change, and the matter was dismissed by a special meeting of the Bar Committee in March 1984 attended by Sir Michael Havers, QC, and leaders of the six circuits. The government remained silent on the matter.

The liability of lawyers for negligence in dealing with clients' affairs is unique among the professions. The normal rule of law for the professions generally is that anyone holding himself out as possessing reasonable competence in his avocation owes a duty to advise with reasonable competence and care. If in breach of that duty the person to whom the duty was owed suffers damage, the professional man is liable to compensate that person for the damage he has suffered. The law, therefore, requires the damage to be borne by the person whose breach of duty caused it, rather than by the innocent person who has suffered it. But this does not apply to barristers.

There remains a strong current belief that a barrister cannot be held liable for negligence because he or she has no contractual relationship with the client and cannot therefore sue the latter for fees. While it is true that barristers cannot sue for their fees, they can demand that their fees be paid before they appear in court. If the barristers do not demand their fees in advance and the lay clients do not pay them after their services have been rendered, the solicitors can sue the lay clients for the barristers' fees.

There exists a peculiar archaic relationship between a barrister and the instructing solicitor. It is said to be founded on tradition and on mutual respect for each other's roles, and much of it is left unspoken. For instance, a solicitor would rarely tell a barrister how his performance might be improved, even if he knew him well, nor would a barrister complain to a solicitor about badly prepared instructions or complain directly to the solicitor about the non-payment or late payment of fees. It is rare that barristers demand their fees in advance, and indeed as solicitors are often unable to pay counsel's fees until the costs of the case have been taxed and paid by their lay client there may be long delays in paying counsel. Nevertheless, by the 'cab rank' rule, barristers are obliged to accept instructions from a solicitor if they are free to do so, even if they have not received fees from the instructing solicitor in connection with a previous case.

This remarkable state of affairs became more ludicrous in 1982 when the Annual General Meeting of the Bar voted overwhelmingly in favour of a resolution to prevent any barrister from acting on behalf of a solicitor or firm of solicitors who had defaulted or delayed payment of counsel's fees. Under the resolution, barristers were prepared to resort to 'industrial action' to recover fees from solicitors (fees that are not legally enforceable). They proposed that solicitors who failed to pay a barrister's fee within three months of demand should be placed on a blacklist. It would constitute professional misconduct for a barrister to accept work from solicitors on the blacklist unless his fee was paid at the outset on delivery of his brief. Later, in a ballot the barristers accepted an alternative scheme proposed by the Bar Council under which a barrister must report a solicitor to the Bar Council for failing to pay his fees unless he has received a satisfactory explanation or has agreed that the fee need not be paid within the normal three-month period. The Bar Council would then endeavour to resolve the complaint with the senior partner or principal of the firm of solicitors and if this failed the Bar Council would refer the complaint to the Law Society. Despite these subtle and effective means of exacting their fees, other than through normal legal channels, barristers continue to lead the public to believe that they provide their services in the expectation of what is virtually an honorarium, not under contract. They claim to be lawyers with no legally precise terms of business, and fees for their work arrive not when requested but only when those who have the honorary duty of paying them care to get round to sending them.

It is clearly illogical for barristers to be granted immunity from a liability for negligence on the basis that there is no contractual relationship between a barrister and his client. Nevertheless, they have been able to retain a large degree of immunity from an action for negligence on the ground that 'public policy' requires it. A barrister's immunity also extends to those pre-trial matters that could be said to be preliminary decisions affecting the way that the case is to be conducted when it comes for hearing. Public policy, in this particular context, has never been clearly defined, and the nearest one can arrive at an explanation for the doctrine is provided by the case of *Saif Ali* v. *Mitchell & Co.* and others (All. E.R. 1978 p. 1033). Firstly, Lord Wilberforce, in an appeal to the House of Lords, referred to a matter being against public policy when it allowed issues previously tried between a client and his or her adversary to be relitigated between client and barrister, which would happen if negligence proceedings were instituted against a barrister. Secondly, all the Law Lords sitting in the case previously mentioned followed the argument in the case of *Rondel* v. *Worsley* (All. E.R. 1969 p. 993) that a barrister had competing duties to the court and to the client and that no liability for negligence could be brought against a barrister for his conduct of a case in court. It seems that their Lordships felt that it would be against public policy for a barrister to be inhibited in court under a possible threat or risk of proceedings for negligence by his client and thus be unable to fulfil his duties to the court.

This argument was carried further. Lord Wilberforce, Lord Diplock and Lord Salmon held that a solicitor acting as an advocate enjoyed the same immunity from negligence claims as a barrister. The lawyers' interpretation of public policy in this matter appears to be tainted with the influence of professional self-aggrandisement. There is no doubt that barristers must exercise finely balanced judgments in the hurly-burly of a trial on matters about which different members of the profession might take different views, but this alone does not set them apart from other professional men. In no profession does common law impose upon those who practise it any liability for damage resulting from errors of judgment unless the error is such as no reasonably well-informed and competent member of that profession could have made. Common law also makes allowance for the circumstances in which professional judgments have to be made and acted upon. The salvage expert and the surgeon may be called upon to make immediate decisions which if in the result turned out to be wrong would have disastrous consequences. Yet neither salvage experts nor surgeons are immune from a liability for negligent conduct of salvage or surgical operations. The absence of immunity for negligence has not disabled members of professions from giving their best services to those to whom they are rendered. There seems to be no reason why the protection of common law for the professions generally should not equally be sufficient protection for lawyers. If a lawyer's negligence in court falls outside this protection and their client suffers as a result, it is only just and equitable that the case in question should be relitigated. It is difficult to appreciate any circumstances in which it can be in the public interest for a person to suffer loss of freedom or any other loss through the negligence of an advocate without having the opportunity to recover damages from the advocate or having the case relitigated. If it is not in the public interest it should in no way be public policy.

The other argument that no liability for negligence against a lawyer should exist in respect of his actions in court – that he owes a duty to the court as well as to his client and that he might be inhibited if such a liability existed – cannot be sustained. The judge, counsels, witnesses and other parties enjoy 'privilege' in all that they say in court. Consequently, no one can take proceedings against any of the officials in court proceedings for the statements they make during the hearing. In very many trials an advocate has attempted to discredit a witness who is in fact an honest member of the public, who has given evidence fairly and to the best of his or her ability. There can be no criticism of the advocate who does so, although the risk of it often works to the disadvantage of law-enforcement officers. For example, a man of twenty years of age was arrested because he produced a knife on a Victoria Line underground train in July 1984 and ran the blade of the knife across an elderly woman's throat until she shook with fear. He shouted and swore at passengers while demanding money. He was released from custody because none of the passengers was prepared to give evidence against him, not only from fear of him, but also from the fear of appearing before a defending advocate whose only method of defence would have been to discredit them.

Advocates' freedom from the slightest inhibition in court is exemplified in the many attempts they have made to discredit the judge presiding in a case. On 17 October 1983, a judge sitting in the Inner London Crown Court accused a barrister acting for the defendants of trying to gain favour with the jury by making attacks on his ability as a judge. He went on to say: 'There is a disastrous undercurrent which is beginning to pervade parts of the Bar. Barristers trying to score points off the Judge, with blazing rows if possible, either with a view to appeal or of currying points with the jury.' While advocates have this degree of immunity to discredit witnesses and indeed the court itself and have immunity from the world generally for the statements they make in court, there seems to be no possible reason for an immunity from a claim of negligence from the client they are purported to be acting for.

The bulk of a solicitor's work is not in connection with court proceedings, as is a barrister's, and therefore in the main solicitors are legally liable if they deal with the affairs of a client negligently. However, in the real world it is difficult for a claimant to proceed successfully against a solicitor. The general public has always felt that the Law Society should remedy grievances suffered at the hands of any of its members, or at least assist the aggrieved person in obtaining damages. The Law Society does maintain a certain control over its members and requires them to submit accounts drawn up in a prescribed manner, showing separately funds held on clients' account and the total liability to clients; the accounts must be certified by professional accountants. If a solicitor makes off with clients' funds or a loss is incurred by the solicitor using clients' money for purposes which the clients never intended, or an Order of Adjudication in bankruptcy is made against a solicitor, the financial loss of the solicitor's clients is made good by the Law Society's Compensation Fund.

However, there has always been a continuous stream of complaints that the Law Society refuses to investigate allegations that certain solicitors are incompetent or negligent. Consequently, in accordance with the Solicitors Act 1974, the Lord Chancellor's Department appointed a Lay Observer, General Allen, as the profession's watchdog. He reported that most complaints were of excessive delays in handling cases involving claims and in the administration of estates. Some quite simple estates had taken more than ten years to wind up. Where there were grounds for complaints of negligence, it was extremely difficult for the complainant to find another solicitor who was prepared to act on his behalf in bringing an action for negligence against one of his professional brethren. As a result of the Lay Observer's suggestion, the Law Society organized negligence panels to help those who wanted to bring an action against a solicitor but could not find another to accept the case.

The Law Society continues to receive hundreds of complaints about solicitors every year. Most of them are about incompetence on the part of a solicitor. In this respect the Society refuses to help the client unless the solicitor's behaviour amounts to professional misconduct, but this leaves a wide field of incompetence uncovered. According to many reports by complainants, when a complaint is made of gross negligence by a solicitor and his client refers the matter to the Law Society, all the complainant receives, after a long delay, is a letter couched in circuitous phraseology advising the complainant to consult another solicitor. A leaflet enclosed with the letter schedules things which the Law Society can do.

A solicitor who has not been paid his or her fees has a right of lien on the client's documents in his or her possession. That means they have the right to retain the documents concerning the matter until their fees have been paid. But when a claim for negligence against a solicitor is made by a client, it is obvious that the client will be reluctant to pay the solicitor for services in respect of which the solicitor has been negligent and which have resulted in loss to the client. In most cases the client is thus effectively prevented from proceeding against the solicitor because of the absence of the documents involved. However, the Administration of Justice Act 1985 provides for the Solicitors Disciplinary Tribunal, an independent statutory body appointed by the Master of the Rolls, to hear complaints of professional misconduct. The same Act also provides for the setting-up of a committee of the Law Society, containing laymen as well as solicitors, which may examine a solicitor's files when a complaint has been made, and order a solicitor to remit or repay part or all of his costs, or to take specific action in the client's interest to put matters right.

However, the Law Society will not give advice to the complainant on how the matter should be dealt with, and this alone successfully discourages the majority of complainants. A persistent complainant will, most probably, eventually be informed of the existence of a local 'negligence panel', consisting of solicitors who are prepared to give a free session of one hour in advising the client on a possible claim for negligence. Thereafter, the claimant is on his own and has to face the formidable defence of the solicitor and his insurance company, which will clutch at any straw to avoid paying compensation, much to the advantage of the solicitor. Consequently, although there are hundreds of complaints against solicitors, few of the complainants can obtain the services of a solicitor and fewer feel capable of pursuing a claim themselves.

In June 1986 the Law Society introduced the Solicitors Arbitration Scheme to reduce the large number of minor complaints against its members. Under the Scheme no claim can be considered without the consent of the solicitor against whom the complaint is made. All claims in respect of overcharging, dishonesty and misconduct are specifically excluded, as are all matters that cannot be determined by an arbitrator from documents alone.

There is obviously a fundamental defect in the system. Firstly, the Law Society is an organization of and for solicitors and is maintained by subscriptions from them. It operates to further their interests with as much zeal as any trade union furthers the interests of skilled craftsmen. Therefore, except in cases of blatant and publicized dishonesty and/or negligence by its members, the Society cannot be expected to discipline them rigorously as an independent organization empowered to do so. As will be seen later, successive governments have permitted the Law Society to operate the legal aid fund, thus creating a far greater anomaly, in that the Society not only protects the interests of its members but also authorizes their employment by others with funds obtained from central taxation. This conflict in the duties of the Law Society appears to have been exacerbated by regulations under the Legal Aid Act 1982 whereby committees of the Society are able to review applications for legal aid refused by the criminal courts.

Of course, if there were few complaints against lawyers and the general public was satisfied with their services, the question of liability for negligence or incompetence would be of little practical consequence. The majority of those who have little contact with the law or lawyers have a very high regard for them, but among those who have had to resort to the services of lawyers on criminal matters, a substantial proportion are dissatisfied. A study of those in three poor London boroughs who had been to a solicitor revealed that one third of them felt that they had not had all the help they needed.

In a study concerning legal advice in connection with appeals, based on interviews with 134 defendants, including 132 convicted persons, there was much criticism of the performance of lawyers. Of course, a convicted person is not the most objective commentator on the quality of his legal representation, but it would be wrong to dismiss such criticisms out of hand, as unworthy of consideration – incompetence in legal representation in criminal cases could have been the main cause of the conviction. Further, of thirteen respondents who had engaged a Queen's Counsel eight would not have recommended the counsel to a friend; of 108 respondents who had instructed junior barristers, seventy-one would not have recommended their counsel to a friend, and of 126 respondents, seventy-two would not have recommended their solicitors to friends. As twice as many respondents would not have recommended their lawyers in criminal matters as would have done so, there appeared to be a considerable vote of no confidence in the legal profession.

However, from various studies that have been undertaken in connection with lawyers' work in non-litigation fields, it appears that more people were satisfied with the work of lawyers than otherwise. The Lay Observer reported that most frequent complaints drawn to his attention were of excessive delays in handling cases involving claims and in the administration of estates. In some cases, he reported, solicitors for the plaintiff took on cases which were too difficult, complex or burdensome for them to handle. To combine the opinions of the public on lawyers' services in connection with both litigation and non-litigation work, a mass observation study, based on a cross-section of the entire population, asked whether respondents were satisfied, fairly satisfied or not at all satisfied with the way in which solicitors handled problems. The observation showed that 62 per cent were satisfied and 23 per cent fairly satisfied, leaving a fairly high proportion of the population dissatisfied. The reasons for the dissatisfactions were in the main inefficiency, undue delay and cost. Apart from the fact that 23 per cent were only fairly satisfied with the services of their lawyers, a dissatisfied minority of 15 per cent is far too high.

The negligence or incompetence of lawyers is therefore important to the community, and the rights of a client against a solicitor or barrister for negligence should be protected by the profession itself. As the Law Society already operates a compensation fund it should also act as arbiter on questions of its members' negligence, with an eventual right for either side to have the matter brought before the court. A similar right should exist for a client to proceed against a barrister for negligence in court or otherwise.

9

LEGAL AID

A lawyer has no business with the justice or injustice of the case he undertakes.

SAMUEL JOHNSON, in Boswell, *Tour to the Hebrides* (1773)

The last forty years have seen the most fundamental changes in the English legal system since the changes brought about on the signing of the Magna Carta. That enactment, among other things, contained the proclamation 'To no one will we refuse, or delay, right or justice'. This ideal was intended to operate for the benefit of the entire populace, but unfortunately, as court procedures became more technical and the administration of justice more complex, the poor and the deprived could not take advantage of that 'right or justice' because they lacked the means to employ those skilled in the law to advise them and to act on their behalf. Indeed, as late as 1926 F. Gurney Champion's *Justice and the Poor in England* contained a draft Bill amending Article 40 of the Magna Carta to exclude all the poor persons in England. During the 1930s Harold Laski, among others, drew attention to the privileged position in law of those who could afford legal representation.

An argument in favour of a comprehensive legal aid system was put very effectively in a memorandum of the National Council for Civil Liberties in 1974 in connection with the extension of legal aid to tribunals as well as to courts. 'The provision of legal aid at any level of the legal system depends upon the principle that no one should be prevented from pursuing or defending his rights by his inability to pay for legal representation.' It was on these lines that numerous earlier thinkers argued the necessity of providing legal representation for all those who could not otherwise afford it. Some form of legal aid was considered to be just and equitable by all progressive sections of society, but hardly one of them, except members of the Law

Society, suggested the means or the system by which the provision of legal aid and advice should be introduced and operated in England.

In response to the general mood of reform, both the Law Society and the Haldane Society (an organization of radical lawyers) set up committees in 1942 to recommend improvements in the English system of legal aid. The Haldane Society proposed that legal aid should be run by a centralized organization ultimately dependent on, though not controlled by, the state. There would be no means tests and everyone was to be entitled to obtain free legal advice, for which solicitors were to be paid fees a little below the ordinary scales. The Law Society wanted legal aid to be applied to all courts and to be available according to a sliding scale of income to assist those not normally regarded as 'poor' who were unable to pay all their legal costs. The work was to be undertaken by those members of the profession who were prepared to do it, and they were to be paid adequately for their services. The Law Society was insistent that the scheme should be run by the profession and not by a government department or by the local authority. It stressed the need for legal aid to be the exclusive field of private practitioners and suggested that a task force of salaried lawyers should operate the advice centres through-out England and Wales.

The Committee of Inquiry set up by the government on Legal Aid and Legal Advice in England and Wales (Cmd 6641) comprised fourteen lawyers and five laymen. It had to consider not only the different schemes proposed by the Haldane Society – free legal advice and aid for all – and the proposals of the Law Society, but suggestions that the entire legal aid and advice service should be operated by a department of salaried lawyers, as well as arguments that it should be based on the services of private practitioners. The government Committee of Inquiry – understandably, since it had a majority of lawyers appointed to it – favoured the system of engaging private practitioners, and indeed it was with great difficulty that the Committee was persuaded that there was any need at all for salaried lawyers in the scheme. However, they were prevailed upon and there was eventually provision for salaried lawyers to be engaged in Advice Centres in the Act of 1949. The Committee recommended a scheme which closely followed the Law Society's suggestions, the main items being:

(1) Both legal aid and legal advice should be made available at the expense of the exchequer.
(2) The two branches of the legal profession participating should receive adequate remuneration.
(3) The service should be extended to a wider income group than those normally classed as poor, but on a sliding scale.
(4) The scheme should be administered by lawyers.

In the evidence before the Committee concerning the last item, the Labour Party considered that a state-administered scheme was not desirable because the state would be directly or indirectly affected by many of the claims for which the scheme would have to provide legal assistance. Political differences might well arise if local authorities were to be held responsible for the advice given. The Association of Municipal Corporations thought that it was not the proper function of local authorities to advise and act on behalf of one ratepayer in private matters involving another ratepayer and it also pointed out that in many cases the local authority would be concerned in the case.

The Committee did make one exception to the general rule that the scheme should be administered by lawyers: criminal legal aid, it suggested, should be dealt with separately and provided by the courts themselves. The Committee recommended that legal aid should be available in all cases in the criminal courts 'where it seems desirable in the interests of justice' and any doubts were to be resolved in favour of the applicant.

When the government introduced the Legal Aid and Advice Bill based on the recommendations of the Committee it was certainly not passed without a great deal of criticism. One lawyer Member of Parliament (Emrys Hughes) said that he thought it a mistake for the scheme to be run as 'a closed shop entirely the preserve of lawyers'. The Bill was described by another Member of Parliament (C. Royle) as 'a set-up between two branches of the legal profession' and yet another member (H. Wallace) said that he hoped some day to hear 'that the Miners' Federation will be given a similar trust in connection with the nation's coal resources'. Attempts were made to secure some lay participation in the administration of the scheme which received very considerable support from the public, but the legal profession protested and by tortuous reasoning claimed that it would make them subject to 'possible' political pressure. Indeed, it is reported that the Law Society told the Lord Chancellor that if the proposals were amended in this manner its members would not participate in the scheme's introduction or serve on the legal aid panels. It seems that the government and consequently the nation were coerced by the legal profession, because a change was inserted in the Bill specifically forbidding any lay participation on the legal aid committees. When the Act was passed in 1949, not surprisingly both branches of the legal profession were delighted. The President of the Law Society pointed out that the government Committee of Inquiry had recommended basically the scheme which the Council of the Law Society had submitted, and the Bar, which was suffering from a shortage of work – the effects of high taxation and post-war inflation – welcomed the Act.

There were delays in implementing the Act and some of the provisions remain in abeyance today. Legal aid was introduced for High Court matters in 1950. Within a few months Lord Singleton discovered that both parties to an action brought before him could be financed by legal aid. He was rather appalled at the number of assisted persons and how many there were likely to be. About a month later the Lord Chief Justice, Lord Goddard, was more pointed in his remarks. He stated that he could not understand why legal aid was granted at the public expense in many of the cases that came before the courts. It was a very serious matter, he went on to say – the country was being put to enormous expense through the granting of legal aid in cases where it should never have been granted at all. Mr Justice Hibling observed: 'The plaintiff brings litigation out of the pockets of all of us, and the money for the defence also comes out of the pockets of all of us. What a luxurious way of litigating!'

The other milestones were that the County Courts participated comprehensively in the scheme in 1956 and the House of Lords, the Magistrates' Courts and the Criminal Courts were incorporated actively in the early 1960s. Despite the urgent representations by the Citizens' Advice Bureau, the component of the 1949 Act relating to salaried lawyers was not implemented. Some five years later a Select Parliamentary Committee investigating the scheme reported that, in the absence of the introduction of salaried lawyers, the system was 'but a truncated version of that envisaged in the Act'. Still nothing was done concerning salaried lawyers and to pacify the increasing demand for easily accessible free legal advice, the government authorized an advice service based on private practitioners' offices known in the profession as the 'pink form scheme' and later the 'green form scheme'. Furthermore, the report of the Royal Commission on Legal Services included detailed proposals for the injection of a salaried lawyers element into the legal aid provisions. But despite the provisions of the 1949 Act and the 1972 and 1974 Acts, the pressure from the Citizens' Advice Bureau, the report of the Select Parliamentary Committee and the Royal Commission on Legal Services, nothing has been done to introduce a department of salaried lawyers into the scheme.

The original scheme of salaried solicitors, operating on a full-time or a part-time basis, never got off the ground, although it would have provided an immediate service in every locality to which any person in need of advice could turn. It would have provided a major bulwark for the ordinary citizen facing the increasingly powerful state. But the legal profession feared that it was the thin end of a dangerous wedge which might lead to restrictions and even to a corps of practising solicitors and barristers being paid a salary. They achieved their aim in preventing the original 1949 statute being fully implemented by suggesting that the appointment of salaried lawyers would endanger civil liberties!

So the position today is that the legal aid system is based on the private practitioners of law, and the government has resolutely refused, and continues to refuse, to introduce departments of salaried lawyers into the scheme. Nevertheless, it placed the legal aid fund (a fund provided by the Exchequer) firmly under the control of the Law Society, without any non-lawyers being present or represented in any stage of its administration. For operational purposes, the Society set up legal aid area committees of its members, with the addition of a representative of the Bar and an officially appointed secretary, to deal with applications for legal aid within that particular area. Yet at the same time the Society was and is a representative body for solicitors, maintained by subscriptions from solicitors and ostensibly democratically controlled by them.

In practice, the position is that any person with insufficient means to institute proceedings himself in court who believes, however tenuously, that he has a civil right against another could initially consult a solicitor for limited advice. The solicitor could then assist that person to make application for legal aid in connection with the problem in question and would make as strong a case as possible for its being granted. The application would be considered by the secretary of the legal aid area committee, himself a solicitor, but he and his committee would have before them only one side of the dispute and that expressed forcibly in the phraseology of a trained lawyer who claimed to be acting in the best interests of his client but who also had a vested interest in the outcome of the application.

Obviously, the secretary and the legal aid committee would not be in a position to pre-judge the issue, but they would have to make a decision on the matter. Unless the proposed action was clearly frivolous or inappropriate, the application could not be refused without casting doubt upon the professional ability of a colleague in private practice. In addition, there is a pronounced possibility that the committee might be influenced, subconsciously or otherwise, by the knowledge that a refusal of the application would result in a loss of work for one of their professional brethren.

Thus the Law Society, a body of solicitors, authorizes work for its members in private practice and authorizes the payment of their fees, including profit costs, out of public funds subject only to taxation (a means by which the court agrees a solicitor's Bill of Costs). This provides the solicitor with the strongest motivation to undertake as much work as possible on a case, whether or not it benefits his client, merely to increase his own profit. This is a position to be envied by every other profession. It would be considered intolerable if a trade union suggested a similar arrangement for itself. The medical and education professions, which function under government schemes and are paid by the Exchequer, have lay members at all levels of their administration.

The result has been that a not inconsiderable number of solicitors with insufficient clients to provide them with the income to which they feel entitled are prepared to join legal aid panels and encourage their legal aid clients to pursue claims to the ultimate, whatever the merit of the case. Their clients have nothing to lose and the solicitors have everything to gain in fees. This has reversed the position that existed hitherto. Before the system of legal aid was introduced into

England, litigation was tilted heavily against those of limited resources. It is now tilted heavily in their favour. Nowadays, prudent
persons of average or above-average income and capital, who do not
qualify for legal aid, must not only consider the prospects of success
before embarking upon litigation but because of the unpredictability
of the outcome must carefully consider whether or not they are in a
position to lose sufficient funds to meet not only their own costs but
possibly the costs of the other side if the proceedings prove to be
unsuccessful.

Lord Denning, Master of the Rolls, in the case of *Chapman* v.
Honing 1963, said that it was a case in which he would certainly in the
ordinary way, on account of its general importance, have given leave
to appeal to the House of Lords, but in view partly of the small
amount of money involved, and, of much more importance, in view
of the present position of the law whereby an unassisted person may
find himself saddled with a great amount of costs which would not
be paid by the legally aided person, he and his colleagues did not give
leave to appeal.

Because of this, and the various judges' warnings of blackmailing
actions by legally assisted persons, the Legal Aid Act of 1964 was
passed. This Act, far from treating successful unassisted litigants
fairly and as entitled to costs from the Legal Aid Fund in what might
be thought to be the ordinary way, introduced considerable discretion
and opportunity for bias on the recovery of costs. Any person claiming
their costs against an assisted person from the Legal Aid Fund (as
provided for in the Legal Aid Act 1964) would first have to prove
that the action was brought by the assisted person. (In other words if
the unassisted person had initiated the action against the assisted
person and was successful, the unassisted person could not recover
his costs.) They would then have to persuade the court that it was
'just and equitable' that costs should be paid from public funds and it
was left to the judge to decide what should be taken into account.
Finally, the court had to be satisfied that the unassisted party would
suffer 'severe financial hardship', without further explaining the
meaning of that phrase. Not surprisingly this Act did virtually nothing
to alleviate the fundamental inequality between the assisted and unassisted litigant.

The memorandum of the National Council for Civil Liberties,

previously referred to, continued as follows: 'We therefore begin from the premise that in the absence of convincing arguments to the contrary, legal aid ought to be made available to those whose rights are at issue in any proceedings before a Court or Tribunal and who cannot, through lack of means, pursue or defend their rights in such proceedings on equal basis with their opponents.' Now unless a person is extremely wealthy he or she cannot pursue or defend their rights on an equal basis with legally aided persons who have unlimited funds behind them.

Legal aid in respect of criminal cases presents problems of an entirely different nature. As we have seen, the criminal courts grant legal aid to defendants, and in charges of murder or appeals by the prosecution to the House of Lords legal aid must be granted and the court must grant legal aid, subject to means, when it appears desirable to do so in the interests of justice. Where there is any doubt whether the granting of legal aid is in the interests of justice it should be decided in favour of the applicant. However, this general test is sufficiently wide to give the courts almost total discretion over whether or not legal aid should be granted in criminal cases other than in cases of murder or in appeals to the House of Lords. There is no obligation on courts to give reasons for refusing legal aid and it is thus impossible to assess whether courts with high refusal rates operate on different criteria from other courts or whether they are exercising their discretion in an acceptable fashion. It is significant that there is an extremely wide difference in the proportion of legal aid applications granted in the Crown Courts from those granted in Magistrates' Courts. In the Crown Courts, all of which are presided over by trained lawyers, the proportion of applications for legal aid granted has always been consistently high – in excess of ninety-nine per cent. Of eighty-seven Crown Courts examined, thirty-two of them granted all applications for legal aid for trial, sentence and appeal.

As the vast majority of the defendants in the Crown Court are represented, most of them on legal aid, and the Crown Court grants the vast majority of applications for legal aid, it would add very little to public expenditure if full legal aid at the Crown Court was granted automatically. Indeed, if this legal aid work was undertaken by salaried lawyers there might well be a saving on the legal aid fund. However, lawyers have not only been reluctant to agree to salaried lawyers acting under legal aid, but they have not accepted the possibility that legal aid should be granted as of right. They are reluctant to consider themselves as providing a service to consumers, let alone consider themselves as a social service. Clinging to the past, they remain the last bastion into which the concept of consumer sovereignty has not penetrated. They have been able to retain eighteenth-century practices and outlook because of the weighty representation which they have enjoyed in both Houses of Parliament and in successive governments. Parliament has therefore been discouraged from introducing radical reforms of the legal system or reforms of the legal professions. Indeed, governments have been persuaded to follow the suggestions of the legal professions, with the notable exception of the abolition of the solicitors' conveyancing monopoly. Even so, this exception was forced upon the government by public opinion and the encroachment on this type of work by conveyancing agencies which were originally operating outside the law.

The granting of legal aid in Magistrates' Courts, most of which are not presided over by professional lawyers, shows an entirely different practice from that in the Crown Courts. In committal proceedings before the Magistrates' Courts approximately seventy-five per cent of defendants are legally aided. In trials in the Magistrates' Courts of indictable offences about fifty per cent are legally aided, and in non-indictable offences, including motoring offences, less than two per cent are represented. In a survey carried out by the Lord Chancellor's Department at fifty-nine Magistrates' Courts during four weeks in December 1982, it was shown that there was considerable variation in the granting of legal aid. Before the survey was commenced it was appreciated that some courts might well be reluctant to grant legal aid in connection with charges for minor offences, and therefore the survey was restricted to about 3,000 cases involving offences of shoplifting, assaulting a police officer, possession of drugs such as cannabis, criminal damage and social security fraud. All five offences could be tried summarily by the Magistrates' Courts or by indictment before a jury, and all of them are considered to be more than minor offences. Of the fifty-nine courts in the survey, only eleven, like the Crown Courts, granted legal aid to every applicant charged with the offences referred to. One court that received twenty-nine applications relating to these offences during the survey period refused all of them. However, the survey demonstrated overwhelmingly that those who received comparatively heavy sentences for the five offences, such as immediate or suspended custody or community service, received legal aid if they asked for it. Nevertheless, the legal profession through the Lord Chancellor intends to introduce, under the powers granted in the 1982 Legal Aid Act, regulations that will allow committees of the Law Society to review applications for legal aid that are turned down by the courts. Thus we return to a similar position as the granting of legal aid in civil proceedings. Either the criminal courts grant legal aid or the Law Society has to deal with the application on review, the outcome of which appears to be predictable.

Indeed, what really concerned the legal profession and appears to have caused it to raise its hands in horror was that the survey revealed that 36 per cent of the defendants who received immediate or suspended custodial sentences or community service did not apply for legal aid. It follows that the legal profession are of the opinion that gone are the days when villains could consider their arrest as a 'fair cop' and would be prepared to accept the consequences of their actions. They must all be rigorously defended, whether they want to be or not. One cannot help wondering whether the eagerness to defend is for the benefit of the prospective clients or the legal profession.

It goes without saying that legal aid based on the private practitioner service has helped to bring unprecedented prosperity not only to the Bar but also to solicitors. It has caused the whole court system to groan under the immense increase in the work load, and despite a substantial increase in the number of judges in the circuits and in the High Court (much to the delight of the Inns of Court) they have been unable to cope with ever-increasing litigation. It has resulted in long delays before matters can be brought before the courts, and in civil proceedings the delays have become so intolerable that out-of-court settlements are arrived at that have no resemblance to what the law intended. Under the present system the lawyers have created more work for themselves and the courts than is necessary or is beneficial for their legal aid clients, and the time has come for a radical reappraisal of the fundamental procedure. If legal aid was operated by salaried lawyers there would be no incentive for them to waste the court's time in order to increase their own income, nor would it benefit them to build false hopes for their clients by persuading them to defend or bring actions that have no real chance of success or to appeal against a sound court decision.

There is nothing new in the suggestion that salaried lawyers can render as efficient a service as lawyers in private practice. A White Paper in 1983 proposed the establishment of a centrally funded national prosecution service, headed by the Director of Public Prosecutions and supervised by the Attorney General. Under those proposals salaried lawyers were to be employed by the national prosecutions service to take over the conduct of all prosecutions from the the police. In 1986 the proposals were put into effect by the Prosecution of Offences Act 1985 without the slightest criticism concerning the efficiency of salaried lawyers from the Law Society. They did suggest that such a service for defendants and in civil proceedings might adversely affect the liberty of the citizen, but at the same time they appeared overtly to recommend the use of salaried lawyers, though it would be restricted to legal advice rather than legal aid, while they covertly opposed such a system.

Because of the inordinate delays in bringing matters before the courts, there has been great dissatisfaction with them as a means of settling disputes involving businessmen, and there is a tendency for a large segment of the industrial and commercial community to abandon the courts and establish their own tribunals of arbitration to settle disputes. Furthermore, in the last fifty years there has been a tendency for most new and vital issues to be left completely in the hands of the executive, and if some adversary procedure was deemed necessary, governments came to prefer flexible policy-conscious administrative tribunals to the more cumbrous and formalistic courts of law. Unless many of the shortcomings in the legal system and legal professions are remedied this tendency is likely to be extended to other areas.

This brings the risk of inequitable practices, and indeed there is great controversy about the scope of 'administrative justice', that is the conferment on a public body, other than a regular court of law, of the power to decide disputes which for one reason or another have been challenged but refer to matters falling within the administrative duties of a section of a ministerial department. The growth of regulatory responsibilities of government has brought about an ever-increasing number of tribunals, but the quality of the decisions they have arrived at has not always been as high as the public might expect.

Simple requirements such as the right to state a case fully, to criticize the opponent's case and to exercise both rights before a more or less impartial adjudicator have not invariably been met. The tribunals have been created as the need for them arose, and their constitution and manner of appointment have varied widely, with no discernible underlying principle. The right of appeal from their decisions to higher authority, such as a law court, a minister, or a superior tribunal, are subject to unpredictable and inexplicable variations. Even the names given to the bodies, tribunals, commissions, courts, committees, referees and so on reflect differences in the bodies. Indeed, the distinction between the advisory and judicial functions of the bodies are never entirely clear.

The continued extension of governmental activity into the affairs of the community has greatly multiplied the occasions on which an individual may be at issue with the administration or with another citizen or body, and much of this judicial business has been confided to tribunals. Therefore, in sheer size and scope, administrative justice now dwarfs law administration of the more conventional and familiar kind. The ordinary citizen is, in fact, far more likely to have to appear before an administrative tribunal or to present a case to be inquired into by a minister than to find himself or herself involved in the machinery of justice as represented by the Magistrates' Courts, the County Courts or the Crown Courts.

10

PUNISHMENT

The object of punishment is, prevention from evil;
it never can be made impulsive to good.

HORACE MANN, *Lectures and Reports on Education* (1845)

However 'just' the law of any state and however fair the application
of the Rules of Law may be, both may be defeated by the state's
treatment of those who have perpetrated offences. If the chances of
apprehending a criminal or of convicting him if caught are remote, he
will probably repeat the crime, particularly if it is one from which he
receives some benefit, such as burglary, robbery with or without
violence, or blackmail. Similarly, if his treatment after conviction is
too light, he will most probably repeat the crime and consider the
punishment as a possible obligation to society which is far outweighed
by the benefit derived from the criminal act. In other words, he
would consider the punishment a not too onerous occupational
hazard.

There is a great deal of disagreement concerning the aims of the
United Kingdom penal system. According to official publications the
aims are to deter the potential lawbreaker and to reform the convicted
offender. The element of deterrence, it is said, is intended to lie in
the fear of detection, the public trial that ensues and the possibility
of punishment, rather than in the severity of the punishment itself.
But this element of deterrence seems to be extremely weak in view of
the ever-increasing crime rate.

The automatic penalty for murder in England and Wales is imprisonment for life – a sentence which may also be imposed for
manslaughter and certain other offences, including rape, robbery
with violence and arson. The death penalty for those offences has
been abolished, and although it may still, in theory, be imposed for
certain offences, such as treason, it is no longer used, despite the
clamour for its implementation against treasonable terrorists.

Except in cases of murder, for which the penalty is prescribed by law, the court has the discretion to select the penalty that it considers most suitable in the light of the nature and gravity of the offence and the information available about the character and needs of the offender. In certain cases this discretion is modified by statutory provisions designed for the most part to ensure that prison sentences are kept to a minimum. Paradoxically, although the courts have imposed more and more alternative penalties to imprisonment for criminal activity, there has been a marked increase in prison population as a result of the rise in crime.

The daily average inmate population of prisons in July 1985 in England and Wales was 48,100, and on the basis of existing trends the population is likely to increase to 49,600 by 1991. The laudable aims of the Prison Rules laid down by the Home Secretary provide for the detention of those committed to custody under the law in conditions generally acceptable to society and for the development of methods of treatment and training which will encourage and assist prisoners to lead a good and useful life. In reality most British prisons were built during the nineteenth century and are now unsatisfactory, insanitary and overcrowded. Although a number of new prisons have been and are being built and existing establishments have been re-developed and modernized, in far too many 'closed' prisons the inmates have to participate in the humiliating and nauseating process known as 'slopping out', that is the removal of human excreta from their own cells to the latrines in procession. This is made worse because in numerous prisons there are four prisoners in cells that were originally intended, a century ago, for one or two.

Prisons to which offenders may be committed directly by the courts are known as local prisons. They are all surrounded by high walls, and windows and doors within the building are barred to restrict the area of the prisoners' activity. The prisoners are classified into groups, according to their record, character and potentialities, and the risk they present to security. They are then assigned, so far as circumstances permit, to the establishment best suited to them. People awaiting trial are entitled to privileges not granted to convicted prisoners and, as far as practicable, are separated from convicted prisoners. Prisoners under twenty-one years of age awaiting trial are separated from older prisoners. The convicted prisoners may be assigned to top-security prisons, ordinary closed prisons or open prisons that do not have physical barriers to prevent escape. On reception under sentence, all persons, except those sentenced to imprisonment for life, are credited with remission of one third of their sentence provided it does not reduce the sentence to less than five days, but remission may be forfeited for serious misconduct. People sentenced to life imprisonment for certain categories of murder, including terrorist murder and the murder of police officers, must serve a minimum of twenty years' imprisonment. There is no remission for prisoners serving sentences under civil law or those serving sentences of unspecified length, such as the criminally insane, whose release depends upon improvement in their mental condition.

Prisoners serving fixed sentences of more than eighteen months become eligible for release on parole after one third of their sentence, or six months, whichever expires later, although there are proposals to discontinue this provision for those serving long sentences for violent and certain other offences. Each eligible prisoner is first considered by a local review committee, which reports to the Home Secretary or the Secretary of State for Scotland on his or her suitability for parole. The Minister concerned then refers a selection of recommendations to the Parole Board for England and Wales or the Parole Board for Scotland, each of which consists of a Chairperson and a number of other members appointed by the Home Secretary and the Secretary of State for Scotland respectively. When the Parole Board recommends favourably, the decision whether or not to release the prisoner depends finally on the Minister, but when the Board does not recommend the release the Minister has no power to grant parole. When granted the parole licence remains in force until the date on which the prisoner would have been released but for the parole. It prescribes the conditions with which the offender must comply. Of those prisoners granted parole in England and Wales 11.4 per cent were recalled to prison in 1982 and in the same year 6.1 per cent of those granted parole in Scotland were recalled.

Prisoners serving life sentences are also eligible for release on licence after consideration by the Home Secretary or the Secretary of State for Scotland, who consults the judiciary. The usual practice in such cases is to seek the views of the local review committee after the offender has served seven years. After each case has been considered by the Home Secretary or the Secretary of State for Scotland it is forwarded to the Parole Board concerned. The Lord Chief Justice in England or the Lord Justice General in Scotland and, if he or she is available, the judge who presided at the trial must be consulted before any life-sentence prisoner is released. In addition there are emergency powers to release offenders in England and Wales up to six months early.

In prison, employment is provided for the prisoners that aims to give them work experience which will assist them on their release. It also aims to secure a return which will reduce the cost of the prison system. In England and Wales prison work is controlled by the Directorate of Industries and Supply of the Prison Department of the Home Office, which comprises executive, professional and technical staff. Technical advice and services to the workshops are provided by visits from headquarters staff. Industrial managers of establishments assist governors with the day-to-day running of the workshops. Farms and gardens attached to penal establishments are controlled by the Chief Farms and Gardens Officer at the Directorate's headquarters.

The primary source of work for prison inmates lies in the requirements of the prison service itself, mainly building and maintenance, domestic services and equipment. Goods and services are also supplied to other government departments and, on an increasing scale, to other purchasers outside the public service. A few prisoners are employed outside the prison in agriculture, work of an archaeological nature, the preservation of canals etc.

Small payments are made to inmates for the work they do, and in some prisons payments above the minimum are made on the basis of output and skill. Any prisoner serving a sentence of four years or more may be considered for employment in an ordinary civilian job outside prison for about the last six months of sentence. During that period the prisoners may live in a separate part of the prison or in a hostel outside. Normal wages are paid, so that the offenders can resume the support of their families and meet their own expenses. Periods of home leave may be granted to assist them with their resettlement.

Education for those in custody in Great Britain is provided by local education authorities. Most prisons have prison education officers assisted by teams of part-time and full-time teachers. Education is compulsory and full-time for young offenders below school leaving age, and in England and Wales there is part-time education for those between sixteen and twenty-one years of age. For older prisoners education is voluntary. They may attend evening classes and take correspondence courses. Depending on the resources available, there are recreational and leisure pursuits such as physical training, concerts, plays, films, lectures and group discussions. Many establishments lack these facilities, and although improvements have been made they fall far short of acceptable standards. However, prisons have libraries, which depend mainly upon local public libraries for their stock. For selected prisoners vocational training courses, leading to an acknowledged qualification such as the City and Guilds of London Institute, and courses preparatory to the examinations of the Open University, are available.

From the beginning of their sentences, all prisoners have a legal right to write and receive letters and to be visited by their relatives at regular intervals. They also have such privileges as additional letters and visits, the use of personal radios, books, periodicals and newspapers, and the right to purchase from the canteen with money earned in prison. Depending on the facilities available at individual establishments, they may be granted the privileges of dining and recreation in association and they may watch television.

The welfare of prisoners is mainly the responsibility of probation officers and assistant governors. They are stationed in prisons to help prisoners in their relationships with individuals and organizations outside the prison and to assist with plans for their aftercare on their return to society. For the spiritual welfare of the inmates, a chaplain of the Church of England, a Roman Catholic priest and a minister of the Methodist Church are appointed to every prison. Ministers of other denominations are either appointed or specially called in as required. Services are held, and soon after reception every prisoner is visited by chaplains, who also visit all prisoners who are sick or confined to their cells and aim to visit all prisoners shortly before their release. Prisoners may also receive visits from specially appointed prison visitors, whose work is voluntary.

Medical attention is provided by full-time and part-time medical officers, whose duties include the care of the physical and mental health of prison inmates. Each establishment has accommodation for sick people, and in a few prisons there are large, fully equipped hospitals where major surgery can be undertaken and treatment by visiting specialists can be given both to inmates and to prisoners from other establishments. Patients, when necessary, can also be transferred to National Health Service hospitals.

In addition to the psychiatric prisons, several prisons have their own psychiatric clinics, to which prisoners from other establishments may be referred. There is also a prison psychological service, whose officers assist governors and medical officers in their work of examining and classifying prisoners. They evaluate treatment programmes, study management practices and contribute to the treatment of individuals and groups.

To a degree, the psychological services and the psychiatric clinics are necessary to treat symptoms created by the prison system itself, and there is a latent risk that the psychiatric clinics could be used as part of the prisons' restricting function by the method of treatment given. There is general consensus among prison staff and prisoners themselves that long-term prisoners, particularly certain indeterminate or life-sentence inmates, become institutionalized. The prisoner becomes excessively and irrationally concerned with the small things of existence and is unable to take in the significance of important changes or misfortunes in the lives of relatives outside the prison. Such prisoners look inward and become selfish. They become less alert, less ready to attempt any new activity, and less able to pursue one if they do take it up. They seem to lose the will or ability to make decisions, and are content to become dependent on someone else to do so for them.

Although there are reasonably reliable and validated tests of depression, hopelessness, a feeling that one is not responsible for one's fate and for what happens to one, neurosis, anxiety and 'effective flattening' (a tendency to respond less to the part of communication that conveys emotion, and to be less interested in the emotional responses of people), there is little that can be done to remedy the complaints effectively.

While the majority of prisoners serve relatively short sentences, there is a population of about 1,500 life-sentence prisoners, mostly convicted of murder or 'diminished responsibility' manslaughter but including ten per cent of other offences. Rather more than a hundred such persons are received each year. They serve between nine and twelve years before release on licence, though a few are released earlier and a small but not insignificant proportion serve much longer.

Occasionally, to some naturally aggressive prisoners, minor incidents can become explosive, and it has been suggested that drugs have been used in prison psychiatric clinics to subdue a trouble-making 'patient' and bring him into line with the institutionalized prisoners. This allegation has been made by several discharged prisoners, but the information provided from that source could not be relied upon without some supporting evidence. This is difficult to obtain. Indeed, it is unlikely to be proved, because the person administering the drug (if it was in fact administered) could claim to be acting on a professional opinion and may honestly believe that the treatment was in the interest of the patient. Nevertheless, the public should always be conscious of the possibility that such treatment may not be in the best interests of the prisoner and could be used against any prisoner who understandably protests against an injustice in prison conditions and causes inconvenience to prison authorities.

The conditions in some of the older prisons in Britain contrast strongly with those in modern prisons such as Wayland, which was opened to receive prisoners in February 1985. The cells, with *en suite* toilet facilities, are designed to accommodate one prisoner and are light, colourful and reasonably comfortable. The communal facilities include extensive equipment for physical education and, as one local authority councillor commented, the prisoners have everything except a golf course. Many people considered that such conditions were far better than those in the National Health hospitals and old people's homes provided by the government and were too good for people who had committed crimes. Others considered the prison to be the result of the government's over-reaction to the years of deplorable conditions under which prisoners had been kept. Until all prisons have been brought up to a reasonable standard, it is the prison authorities who allocate prisoners to the various establishments who determine the type of sentence served – the judges and the courts merely determine its length. This is not only wrong but unjust, because if two criminals given the same sentence for identical crimes were in the opinion of the judge to be treated in the same way, they should both be given the same conditions in which to serve their time.

*

There are a variety of non-custodial means of dealing with a person found guilty of a criminal offence. An absolute discharge or conditional discharge may be granted when the court considers that there is no need to impose punishment. Or offenders may be 'bound over' – that is to say, required to pledge money, with or without security, 'to keep the peace and be of good behaviour'. Or they may be fined a specified sum of money or be placed on probation, which is designed to rehabilitate them. They continue to live an ordinary life with the supervision and assistance of a probation officer. Before making a probation order, which in England and Wales lasts between six months and three years, the court proposing to make the order must explain its effects and make sure that the proposed probationer understands that failure to comply with it will make him or her liable to be dealt with again for the original offence. An offender must be seventeen years of age or over and must have given consent before such an order can be made. It usually requires the offender to keep in regular touch with the probation officer, and to be of good behaviour. In England and Wales the probation service is administered locally by probation and after-care committees of local magistrates and co-opted members with legal and specialist interests. The committees may provide and maintain day training centres, probation hostels and other rehabilitation centres. They also administer the community service scheme (referred to below). The services of the probation and after-care officers are available to assist every criminal court.

When a court in England or Wales feels that it has no alternative but to pass a sentence of imprisonment, the judge is free to suspend a sentence of not more than two years, in which case the sentence is not served unless the offender is convicted of a further offence punishable with imprisonment. In that event the suspended sentence normally takes effect and another sentence may be imposed for the later offence. An offender receiving a suspended sentence of more than six months may be placed under the supervision of a probation officer for all or part of the period. The courts also have power to order that any sentences between three months and two years should be partly served and partly suspended.

Alternatively, if the offender is aged sixteen years of age or over and is convicted of an imprisonable offence, the court is empowered to make a community service order. However, before such an order can be made the offender must give his or her consent to the order being made. Under the provisions the court may order between forty and 240 hours of unpaid service to be completed within twelve months if the offender is over seventeen years of age and between forty and 120 for those under seventeen years. Community service includes house decorating for the aged or the disabled and building adventure playgrounds.

In England and Wales the courts may order an offender to pay compensation for personal injury, loss or damage resulting from the offence that he or she has committed.

Offenders aged seventeen to twenty years of age in England and Wales are recognized as a category distinct from child and adult offenders. The custodial sentences available are detention centre orders for males from three weeks to four months and youth custody sentences for both sexes. Detention centres provide a means of training, and are intended to deter from further crime young offenders for whom a long period of residential training does not seem necessary but who cannot be taught respect for the law by such methods as fines or probation. The regime of the detention centres is brisk and firm, with strong emphasis on hard work and high standards of behaviour. They provide a normal working week of forty-four hours, including one hour daily devoted to physical training, and considerable attention is paid to education. Young offenders are eligible for parole on a similar basis to adults and all are supervised after discharge.

However, courts may impose custodial sentences only when no other measure is appropriate. A number of alternatives to custody are open to the courts: it may make community service orders or it may order the young offenders to report to Attendance Centres. Those ordered to attend must do so during their spare time on Saturday mornings or afternoons. They may be required to attend for up to three hours on any one occasion and for a total of not less than twelve hours and not more than twenty-four hours. The activities include physical training and instruction in handicrafts or some other practical subject. Efforts are made at the centres to induce the offenders to join a youth club or other suitable organization. The courts may also attach conditions to probation orders.

Changing views of society on how best to deal with the problem of children in trouble have brought about radical changes in England and Wales. No child under ten years of age can be held guilty of an offence. A child aged ten years to sixteen years who is alleged to have committed an offence may be subject to criminal proceedings or to 'care proceedings', both of which normally take place in juvenile courts. In care proceedings the fact that a child is found guilty of an offence is not in itself sufficient justification for making an order. The court must also consider that the child is in need of care or control which he or she is unlikely to receive unless an order is made. In criminal proceedings the court may make a care order without having to consider whether the child needs care or control. This applies to a child found guilty of an offence punishable in the case of an adult by imprisonment.

The principal orders available to the juvenile courts in England and Wales in both care and criminal proceedings are: (a) an order requiring a parent or guardian to enter into a recognizance to take proper care of the child or young person and to exercise proper control over him or her, (b) a supervision order, under which a child will normally remain at home under the supervision of the local authority or a probation officer, (c) a care order, which commits the child to the care of the local authority, and (d) a hospital or guardianship order in accordance with mental health legislation. For children too severely disturbed or disruptive to be treated in local authority homes, there are special Youth Treatment Centres.

The authority must review each care order every six months and consider whether an application should be made to the court to rescind the order, which normally expires when the child reaches eighteen or nineteen years of age. The courts have the power to make a residential care order when a child who is already under a care order as a result of an offence commits a further offence for which an adult could be punished by imprisonment.

The courts may also order payments of compensation, impose fines or grant a conditional or absolute discharge. When a fine, compensation or costs are awarded against a juvenile offender the courts generally order that the parent or guardian should pay.

Juvenile offenders, both male and female, may be ordered to spend a total of up to twenty-four hours of their spare time on Saturdays at an Attendance Centre, and boys aged fourteen to sixteen years of age many be sent to a junior Detention Centre, where the regime is similar to that in senior Detention Centres.

Boys and girls may also be sentenced to a term of youth custody. In the case of a very serious crime, detention in a place approved by the Home Secretary may be ordered.

With such a wide variety of penalties for crime and such wide variations of the treatment of criminals it is not surprising that the sentencing of criminals is and has been subject to considerable criticism. There is, however, general agreement that for murder the mandatory penalty of life imprisonment is right and should remain. Of those who do not agree with life imprisonment, the largest section advocate the death penalty for murder. It therefore appears that there is a consensus of opinion that punishment can really serve to protect a community from similar acts in the future and at the same time act as an expiation of the past action. This stems from the subconscious belief that there is a degree of social morality and social order common to all members of a particular society that plays a major part in the general integration of that society. When the action of an individual or group contravenes that morality and order, it tends to shock the community. When this occurs in animal groups or in primitive human communities vengeance is swiftly inflicted on the culprits. While the vengeance may be a mechanical and aimless reaction or an emotional or irrational movement, it tends to eliminate the menace to the community. It is an act of defence of the norms of the group or community. Punishment for crime through the ages, and even in modern civilized societies, is at least in part a work of vengeance. Although in the United Kingdom the criminal offender is not made to suffer just in order to make him suffer, it is generally felt that it is right that he should suffer. This is reflected in the precautions taken in law, that the criminal should suffer in proportion to his crime, a typical example of which is the mandatory life sentence for murder.

There are those that argue that criminals should be dealt with by means other than imprisonment and that vengeance and punishment should play no part in the effort to re-educate and rehabilitate those that offend society. However, when such theories are embodied in the law or in legal practice, or when the punishment of wrongdoers becomes subservient to the amount of resources the national treasury is prepared to appropriate to the penal treatment of prisoners, the cohesion of society is put at risk. Inevitably, the number of crimes increases dramatically, as more and more people feel that society is prepared to tolerate crime. If the benefit wrongdoers enjoy from crime outweighs the social obligations imposed upon them by non-custodial sentences by the courts, there would be no incentive for them, on economic or social grounds, to mend their ways. The only deterrent to them would be the possibility of their intended victim retaliating effectively. Consequently, the weaker members of society, the aged and the infirm, become at risk and prone to cruel assaults for material gain, or in some instances for 'the hell of it', by the younger, stronger and fitter.

It is paradoxical that in modern society, although the police are not omnipresent, if such weaker members of society arm themselves for self-defence, they may be prosecuted for carrying an offensive weapon. Indeed, if they injure a criminal in the execution of a crime, it is invariably the persons who successfully defend themselves who are brought before the courts for taking the law into their own hands, not necessarily the person intent upon committing the crime.

It seems therefore that the judges and magistrates in England and Wales carry a heavy burden in having to choose what they consider to be the most suitable treatment for each offender coming before them while the law provides for such a wide range of sentences. Research has shown that some judges and magistrates are using prison sentences far more frequently than are others, and that this cannot be fully explained by the fact that they have a larger proportion of people appearing before them who are more likely to be imprisoned by any court. On the other hand, there are other judges and magistrates who imprison far fewer people than can be explained by the type of offender coming before them. However, the great majority of the courts imprison a proportion of people somewhere between these limits, and a small sample of these courts show that they imprison similar types of people. The basic hindrance to gaining equality in sentencing practices seems to lie with the judges and magistrates themselves. They vary in their philosophy of punishment and its aims, and they vary in their belief in the abilities of particular methods of treatment or punishment to achieve the aims they have in mind. Unfortunately, there are no means by which particular judges or magistrates can know the extent to which their particular sentencing has been a success or failure.

At the same time, judges and magistrates are conscious from communications from the Home Office of the desire of that department that sentences of imprisonment be restricted to a minimum and they are mindful of the inadequacy of resources and the consequent overcrowded conditions in penal establishments. Moreover they are frequently in difficulty when sentencing mentally ill offenders when there are no vacancies in institutions in which the mentally sick could receive suitable treatment.

11

THE EVALUATION OF A
LEGAL SYSTEM

'If the law supposes that,' said Mr Bumble, 'the law is a ass
– a idiot.'

CHARLES DICKENS, *Oliver Twist* (1837–9)

To evaluate a legal system it is first necessary to determine the
purpose it is intended to fulfil. Although this statement may be
considered naïve, there remain very significant differences between
the objectives of the legal systems in states that are avowedly democratic and those that are totalitarian, whether communist or fascist.
These systems form polar points on a continuum that contains a wide
spectrum of governmental forms, many of which do not fit easily into
either of the polar camps. It is exceedingly difficult to categorize them,
but if all the members of a political community can be said to govern
themselves, the form of government is democratic. However, if the
community is governed by a single person, or by a small number of
people, it might constitute an absolute monarchy, a one-man dictatorship, an oligarchy, an aristocracy or some other authoritarian system.

All these types of government may exercise varying political authority over the lives of the respective people and society. If this authority
is in principle expected to extend to everything in the lives of the
people, the system is totalitarian. If, on the other hand, the
government is limited, leaving certain, often large, spheres of individual and group life unregulated and guaranteed by law, or protected
by convention, against government intervention, the polity is said to
be 'liberal'. Although most English men and women consider themselves, in the light of this definition, to be living in a liberal democracy, such a definition is subject to historical change and qualification. Most *laissez faire* liberals of the mid nineteenth century (and
those who echo their views) would regard the degree of governmental
regulation and intervention, especially in the field of the economy

and industrial relations, that exists today in 'liberal democratic' countries as totalitarian.

Liberal democracies are characterized institutionally by limitations on government action that provide safeguards for individuals and groups in the community. This means not only that there are private spheres in which government must not interfere, but also that the government's agents, like private persons, must abide by the rule of law and exercise authority only to the degree the law permits. Moreover, public policies must be open to review by the people, who must have the opportunity to analyse issues and criticize government activities. Furthermore, the press, radio and television must be permitted the independent purveyance of news because freedom of speech, like freedom of association and freedom of assembly, are essential basic civil rights.

The effective functioning of a liberal democracy requires not only institutions and guarantees, but also attitudes. Respect for the right of people to assert their point of view, however unpopular or seemingly wrongheaded, is fundamental to the working of the democratic process of discussion and choice. Britain acquired these institutional qualities because of two processes operating at different periods of time. The first was one of differentiation of functions which had originally emanated from the person of the monarch, and subsequently the process of limiting his powers. This long process led to the Magna Carta in 1215, to the separation of the jurisdiction of the courts of law and to the Petition of Rights in 1623 and the Bill of Rights in 1689, which attempted to prevent the monarch from acting in what was considered an arbitrary fashion, destroying customary rights. It was the House of Commons, with its two-fold influence, as a grantor of money and as a representative body, that assumed the leading role in attempting to limit the monarch. And the execution of Charles I made it quite clear that royal power could never again be supreme. However, quite a different process began in the mid eighteenth century, when the king started to select his chief advisers or Ministers from persons who had the confidence and support of a majority of the members in the House of Commons. As this principle became established, the reasons for limiting the powers of the king disappeared. The British Cabinet not only wielded the former powers of the Crown, but possessed a wide measure of independent executive authority, as well as power as the leaders of the legislative body.

The latter leadership was derived not only from the traditional two-party system, which ordinarily guarantees majority party control in the House of Commons, but also from what was formerly the Crown's right to dissolve Parliament which devolved upon the Prime Minister. In a televised Richard Dimbleby Lecture, Lord Hailsham, the Lord Chancellor, claimed that the system constituted an elected dictatorship. However, although the British Cabinet is one of the most powerful executive bodies in the democratic world, it nevertheless in theory accepts a responsibility to act for the country as a whole, and not merely as the organ of the majority party. The courts in Britain do not question the validity of an Act of Parliament, but in their decision-making they proceed from the premise that legislation is meant to be reasonable in intent and to deal fairly and equally with all people. They also have a bias towards the individual freedom of common law, out of which have emanated the basic rules of procedure and their application.

Thus the most decisive factor in maintaining a democratic system is the limitation of the power of government, and that involves an independent judiciary, which protects the rights of individuals and ensures that state action does not transgress constitutional limits, whether written or otherwise. But to what extent the judiciary in England and Wales is independent is debatable. Justice under the law must after all be dispensed by human beings, and they, however strong their feelings of independence and security, inevitably have preferred ideals and predilections, preconceived ideas and prejudices. These may be no more than slight variations from normal but they could be dangerous if they were to lead to the abridgement of basic liberties. Moreover, the law itself necessarily reflects class interests, economic interests and, where particular denominations or churches predominate, religious interests. However, the remedy, if one is desired, is not a change in the judicial system, but a change in the laws through democratic processes.

It may be that the arguments of those that claim that the decisions of British judges are influenced by the political opinions of the government are not without foundation, but there is an additional safeguard against this that manifested itself in the case of Clive

Ponting. He was a civil servant who was tried in the Central Criminal Court in February 1985 under the Official Secrets Act for disclosing information to an opposition Member of Parliament when he thought that the Cabinet was misleading the House. Originally, when his action was investigated by the police, it is alleged that they were of the opinion that no serious breach of security had been committed and no proceedings, at that stage, were envisaged. It was further alleged that his senior officers in the Civil Service were prepared to accept his resignation to terminate the unfortunate matter. However, it was suggested that members of the executive and their political masters were so aggrieved and embarrassed by the disclosure that they pressed for a prosecution.

In the event the trial judge, Mr Justice McCowan, ruled that the defendant's claim that he acted out of 'duty in the interests of the state' was no defence under section 2 of the Official Secrets Act, and this decision was in accordance with the opinions of those who brought the prosecution. Before the jury was selected the Attorney General forwarded to the head of the vetting section of the Security Service MI5 (known officially as C3) the names of sixty men and women chosen at random to form the jury panel. Checks were then carried out to establish whether any person included in the panel was a member of, or sympathizer with, any subversive party or organization. In this context 'subversive' extended to members of the Labour Party believed to be associated with Militant Tendency and other 'extremists' in the party. The checks were supplemented by discreet inquiries among the panel members' colleagues, workmates, neighbours and friends with the aim of compiling a dossier on the person's political and social activities, his standing in the community and so forth. In this area, a man or woman's association with a 'peace movement' or with 'industrial militancy' might be sufficient to exclude that person from the jury. Nevertheless, the jury eventually selected was not satisfied with the prosecution's case and, much to the astonishment of the political establishment, they acquitted the defendant.

Most states, and certainly not only Britain and the United States of America, claim to have a completely independent judiciary. It is claimed that the judiciary in the Union of Soviet Socialist Republics is completely independent of the Communist Party, and to a degree it is. The supervision of the administration and justice in the USSR is done mainly by a special agency, the Procuracy. The Procurator-General is appointed by the Supreme Soviet for a term of seven years and when appointed the Procurator's office is fully centralized. Although branches exist down to the district level, they are not subject to any control from the republican governments or from local soviets. Furthermore, they are designed to be immune from local party influence. The basic Soviet court is the People's Court, which is established at district level. A People's Court consists of a judge (elected by universal suffrage for a term of five years) and two lay assessors (elected by general meetings of industrial, office and professional workers, peasants and servicemen and women for a term of two years). Higher-level courts are elected by the appropriate soviet – the republican Supreme Soviets in the case of the republican Supreme Courts and by the USSR Supreme Soviet in the case of the USSR Supreme Court. The Communist Party does not maintain separate law courts any more than it keeps separate police forces, and party rules provide for the expulsion of a party member for the commission of an offence punishable by a court of law and for prosecution in conformity with the law. It has been laid down by the Central Committee of the Communist Party of the Soviet Union that local party organs must never interfere to influence court decisions. Some years ago the President of the USSR Supreme Court declared: 'No one man is entitled to dictate to the judges their decision in any criminal law case. Neither the agencies of government nor of administration, nor those of the Ministry of Justice, nor social organizations, must interfere with the decisions of individual courts. The interference of local party organs with the decisions of the court cases violates the principle of independence of judges established by the USSR constitution.' However, even the Supreme Court accepts guidance and direction from the Central Committee of the Communist Party of the Soviet Union.

While it is clear that the British judiciary is not subject to the same governmental 'guidance and direction' as the Soviet Union judiciary, the Soviet system does exhibit how loose the term 'independent' can be when attributed to the judicature.

Having dealt briefly with the judicial system acting as a mechanism to protect the individual from the state, we come to the state's duty to maintain order within its boundaries. Heinrich von Treitschke, in his *Politics* (1916), defined the primary duty of the state as 'the double one of maintaining power without, and the law within'. The state's first obligation he thought 'must be the care of its army and its jurisprudence, in order to protect and restrain the community of its citizens'. Earlier Adam Smith had said the same thing: 'The state is concerned externally with defence and internally with justice.' From the individual's point of view Thomas Hobbes in the seventeenth century observed: 'Everyone in a state of nature fears for his safety, and each is out to injure the other before he is injured himself. Finding life in a state of nature impossible, man turned to the state to find the security collectively that they are incapable of finding individually.'

Thus the entire community looks to their government to maintain order within its country, but in a liberal democracy public order seeks to reconcile the conflicting demands of freedom of speech and assembly with the preservation of peace within the state. In Britain, the oldest liberal democracy, a satisfactory balance between those competing aims has rarely been achieved. There has always been the daily task of combatting drunken and disorderly behaviour, brawls and various forms of hooliganism and although it has not attracted a great deal of publicity, it has always been the greatest regular drain on police resources in the area of public order. Other regular disorders have been demonstrations aimed at drawing attention to some cause or other and at achieving maximum publicity. Indeed, some of the controversial cases of public order have arisen from the prosecution of people taking part in them or organizing them. The more one demonstration gains publicity, the more others are encouraged to demonstrate in favour of their 'pet' cause.

Over the past three centuries disturbances and riots have led to the introduction of a surprising complexity of laws concerning public order, and today they appear to be wide enough to meet any possible contingency. These riots were not isolated occurrences. At the beginning of the eighteenth century, there were riots for all sorts of reasons – in connection with witch hunts, public executions, religious feelings, smuggling, press gangs, economic changes and so on. They were, in the main, spontaneous and unorganized. Grievances concerning bread prices, turnpikes and press gangs festered and accounted for persistent outbreaks of similar disorder throughout the eighteenth century. The most notable were those associated with John Wilkes and those known as the Gordon Riots.

The start of the nineteenth century saw the continuance of the old-style spontaneous riots, but it also began to experience organized outbreaks of violence and disorder, to which the government reacted fiercely. Between 1810 and 1820 there were the machine-breaking activities of the Luddites, the march of the Blanketeers, the Peterloo massacre, the Pentrich revolution and the Cato Street conspiracy. The government rigorously suppressed the disorder to frustrate revolutionary tendencies, particularly as the spectre of the French revolution loomed large in the minds of those in authority. Because of economic conditions, another wave of discontent and riots occurred in the 1830s from Staffordshire to Hampshire, when cries of 'Bread and Blood' were raised. Serious riots in London were attributed to 'recent events in France', but the struggle over the Reform Bill also contributed a great deal to the unrest. Particularly alarming were the Bristol riots, which occurred soon after the House of Lords rejected the Reform Bill in October 1831. In 1839 there was a serious outbreak of rioting in Birmingham followed by a treasonable rising in Newport. In west Wales agrarian discontent resulted in the troublesome Rebecca riots of 1842-4.

In that era riots could start at any time and any place for many different reasons. The Sunday Trading riots were a response to Sabbatarian legislation then before Parliament, the Hyde Park riot of 1866 was a product of the Reform Bill movement, and at local levels there were riots as a result of resentment of the Salvation Army, the Mormons and many other religious groups. A common source of disturbance was hostility towards Irish labourers. The riots at Camborne, Cornwall, in 1882 after an attempt to stone two Irishmen in the custody of the police were symptomatic of the trend. In the same year there were serious riots in Tredegar, in which a large number of houses belonging to the Irish were attacked and many of the inhabitants injured. They were followed by the famous Trafalgar Square riots, which sprang from unemployed agitation and later from organized political protests in 1886 and 1887.

The twentieth century began with numerous outbreaks of disorder associated with pacifist meetings during the Boer War and they were followed with riots and disturbances because of the severe industrial unrest. From 1910 until the outbreak of the First World War the militant activities of the suffragettes and other movements made it an explosive time. After the war there were long series of disorders throughout the country due to the plight of the unemployed. The 1930s was a most volatile period. There were serious disorders following the implementation of the government economies from 1931. According to a left-wing newspaper, between 1931 and 1933 a total of 1,432 'workers' were prosecuted because of their fight against the government, of whom 480 were said to have been gaoled, 734 fined, 130 bound over and the remainder acquitted. But it was a period in which public order was also threatened by frequent clashes between political factions, especially between the communists and the fascists. Eventually, the Public Order Act of 1936 was introduced in an effort to reduce the likelihood of such clashes.

A short period after the Second World War was relatively quiet, but the late 1950s saw the advent of the nuclear disarmament movements with their demonstrations, the revival of the various fascist groups and the resultant political clashes, though they were not as serious as those of the 1930s. The 1960s brought the clashes of the 'mods' and 'rockers' and they were followed in the 1970s by the ethnic riots of Brixton in London and St Paul's in Bristol, and by the Toxteth riot in Liverpool. The same period was also marked with the continual industrial unrest that culminated in the miners' disturbances of 1984–5. This brief outline of the disturbances in the history of England and Wales ignores the explosive activities of nationalist organizations that have spread from Northern Ireland from time to time.

Nowadays, the vast majority of trials for crimes involving public order are held in the Magistrates' Court. Although this seems to reflect the traditional involvement of Justices of the Peace in the preservation of the Queen's Peace and indicates that difficult points of law rarely arise in this field, the most likely reason for the reliance on summary trials in public order cases is the need, after outbreaks of disorder, to deal with large numbers of defendants promptly and effectively. Of course, in certain instances the prosecuting authority may decide to proceed by indictment before a judge and jury, and indeed in some instances the defendant might elect for a trial before a jury. In bygone days, those brought before the court experienced remarkable savagery in penalties after a trial by jury. Several Luddites were sentenced to death at the York Assizes in 1813 and the agrarian disturbances led to cruel punishments involving the full severity of the law. Later, by the second half of the nineteenth century, higher courts no longer had the authority or the inclination for such severity, and many of the public order crimes created by statute were made triable at summary level.

Even today, a trial on indictment opens up the possibility of heavier sentences, but on the other hand it enables an accused person who fears bias on the part of the local magistrates, or otherwise distrusts them, to seek trial before a jury. Despite the recent reaction against summary trial and despite a certain attractiveness of trial by jury, the Magistrates' Courts still dominate the judicial enforcement of public order. Those offences that can be tried only on indictment, the common law offences of riot, rout, unlawful assembly and causing an affray or public nuisance are now rarely involved. The common charges in instances of disturbances are: obstructing the police in the execution of their duty, obstructing the highway, and threatening or abusive behaviour, all of which are dealt with summarily. Trials on indictment, when they do occur, are usually sought because the prosecuting authorities take a grave view of the occurrence and wish to secure either an exemplary conviction or an exemplary sentence.

In addition to the common law offences arising from disturbances of the peace, the law of public order is based on the cumulative result of preceptive enactments to meet the peculiar problems connected with the various disturbances previously referred to. Consequently, the law of public order has become extremely vague. The extent to which an incident constitutes a riot or sedition under common law is uncertain, and many modern statutory crimes, such as the use of threatening, abusive or insulting words or behaviour, are not clearly defined in their scope. In most circumstances, therefore, prosecutors in the courts are virtually certain of success. The real choice rests with the prosecutor, firstly in deciding whether the incident is serious enough in his or her mind to mount a prosecution, and secondly in deciding the nature of the charges to be laid when in most cases they could fall within the scope of a number of offences ranging from serious common law charges to those dealt with summarily.

On 13 November 1986 the House of Commons ordered the Criminal Justice Bill (2) to be printed. It proposed that where an offence of, or related to, criminal damage is alleged and it appears to a Magistrates' Court that the values involved do not exceed £2,000 the court is required to proceed as if the offence charged were triable only summarily. The Bill also provides that common assault and battery (common assault under section 47 of the Offences Against the Person Act 1861 and certain other Acts) shall be summary offences. Although these provisions ensure that those who are alleged to have committed the vast majority of public order offences are brought before the court within a day or so of the alleged incident, more by design than accident they deprive the person being charged of the right of trial by jury. They do not however prevent the prosecution proceeding by indictment under other statutes.

Hence, many allegations of political or other discrimination in the sphere of public order have been directed not against the courts, although magistrates and judges have had their fair share of criticism, but against the prosecutors – the police or the government. This is not a recent phenomenon. Throughout history there have been confident allegations of partiality in the process of selecting cases to bring before the courts. It was particularly so in the stormy years when the Salvation Army faced its hooligan opponents, the Skeleton Army, in towns throughout the land, and a few years later when pacifist meetings during the Boer War were attacked and broken up by loyalist groups. In the 1920s and 1930s there were many allegations of unfairness towards the left in their opposition to fascist organizations. The difficulty was expressed during a debate in the House of Commons on anti-Jewish activities in the East End of London by the then Home Secretary, Sir John Simon: 'If this is indeed a free country and we are a free people, a man is just as entitled to profess the fascist philosophy as any other, and he is perfectly entitled to proclaim it and expound it so long as he does not exceed the reasonable bounds that are set by law.'

Very often the complaints are against the actions of the police at the scene of the disturbances rather than against the subsequent decision to undertake a particular prosecution. This is not only evidenced in recent industrial disturbances. As far back as 1937 some Labour Party Conference delegates specifically claimed that the police were discriminating in favour of the fascists. At the same time the fascist organizations were arranging their 'own protection' because the police were unable or unwilling to protect their meetings and assemblies from unruly mobs. It seems therefore that in any public disturbance involving two or more factions, in which the police endeavour to keep the 'peace', whether the factions are differing political groups, management and workers, or differing religious sects, they can be subjected to criticism if they partially thwart the intentions of any or all of the factions. The criticisms in most instances are unjustified, but there are many cases in which a varying degree of bias can be suspected. But this will always be so while there is freedom of speech and assembly in a state that contains two or more conflicting groups whose strong feelings against one another have burst into physical hostility.

The greatest danger may arise if one particular group involved in disturbances recruits so many members as to be too large for the regular police force to deal with. History has shown that those prepared to resort to physical violence are prepared to use any weapons that come to hand to further their cause, and rioters in Toxteth used petrol bombs against the police and property. Various other weapons have been used in industrial disputes, but the police have been expected to contain these outbreaks armed only with outdated truncheons and handcuffs. These were quite adequate in the last century, particularly because of the stature of those recruited to the police. Some of the county police looked a formidable body of men, and indeed the Glamorgan police were well known not only in their own county but as far afield as Cornwall for their ruthlessness in dealing with disturbances.

According to Herbert Spencer, 'Policemen are soldiers who act alone; soldiers are policemen who act in concert.' While this may have been true in his time, the concept of a policeman's duty has changed over the years. The ordinary police constable became the symbol of order as much as the enforcer of order. The only assistance that the police had in crowd control was from their mounted colleagues and from their own dog handlers; they could never call upon the military for assistance to quell a disturbance. Indeed, the last occasion that the military was used in any industrial dispute was between the two world wars, and nowadays the use of the military in such matters has become an anathema to both the public and the authorities. But the degree of violence in public disturbances has escalated during the last two decades and it has been deemed necessary for the police to be supplied with riot shields, 'plastic bullets', CS gas and firearms with more lethal ammunition. Nevertheless, the police themselves are reluctant to use such weapons, and although plastic bullets and CS gas were available to them during the Tottenham riot in 1985, when several of their officers were injured and one was put to death, they refused to use them on the streets of London.

However, a section of the police known as D11 has received special training not only for riots but also to counter terrorist attacks and sieges. They have been armed with percussion grenades and automatic weapons and they now patrol the larger airports fully armed. This change of the police from its traditional peace-keeping role to a counter-attacking force has been condemned by many Chief Constables and notably by John Alderson, the former Chief Constable of Devon and Cornwall, who has rigorously opposed it. Some have argued, with justification, that the image of the police is being destroyed and they have suggested the formation of a completely separate mobile para-military organization to be used in any part of the country when the regular police force in a locality find that a disturbance has gone beyond their control. Such an organization, it is argued, would be trained for the total defence of the country for both external and internal purposes. In addition to assisting the regular police forces it could release all regular and territorial armed forces for overseas duties when necessary. These opinions have varying degrees of support based on the value judgments of those concerned.

It is clear that in a liberal democracy minorities cannot be permitted to get their own way by using force either against the majority or against any other minority within the community. No group is entitled to take the law into its own hands to suppress the activities of others or to impose its own policies on the community, but the extent to which any group is entitled to protect itself from any other group is subject to a great deal of argument. So also is the right of the individual in a liberal democracy to defend himself and his property. Individuals not only look to the state to provide the machinery to limit all claims against them, save those authorized by law, and to provide a force strong enough to keep the peace by quelling all riots and disturbances in the community; they also require the state to provide them with adequate protection from other individuals by providing adequate laws, efficient courts and sufficient police to prevent crimes being perpetrated against them.

In recent years the British government has failed to provide the services of law and order to the level of the expectations of the British public. Crimes against the aged involving violence and robbery are on the increase and in various areas people are afraid to venture out at night because of the immense increase in 'mugging'. There is an increase in all types of violent crimes, and people are being robbed, abused and mutilated in their own homes. Although the law is unable to protect all the people at risk, it does not permit them to defend themselves against criminals on the grounds that they 'should not take the law into their own hands'. Indeed, if they did defend themselves or their property they would be considered criminals, as demonstrated in a case of a shopkeeper being charged with assault as late as 1985. It seems that the shopkeeper had been burgled on no less than eight occasions within a short period of time and when yet another, the ninth, intruder entered his shop and home he defended himself and his property by wielding an iron bar. He inflicted limited injuries on the intruder and later called the police. He was charged for inflicting bodily harm on the would-be burglar, but fortunately when the matter came before the court, it showed a great deal of common sense and he was discharged. Even the intended burglar, who was also charged by the police, agreed that his attacker was justified in his actions. Nevertheless, the shopkeeper had to suffer the indignity of being brought before the court, with all the trauma that entails, merely because he defended his own property, something that the police were unable to do for him. The police are continually warning people not to 'have a go' at criminal attempting a crime, and some judges have suggested that rape victims should submit rather than repel the attacker. So strong is the feeling that people should not take the law into their own hands that girls walking after dark carrying hat pins but not wearing a hat have been charged with carrying offensive weapons.

Although the police have a duty to impose the law, they should exercise considerable discretion when people defend themselves in a reasonable manner. If they cannot or will not do so, the government should either introduce the necessary legislation to enable ordinary citizens to defend themselves and their property or recruit sufficient police.

Indeed, in its international relationships the government claims that its nuclear weapons act as a deterrent against war and that a well-armed nation reduces the risk of an attack from a foreign state. If this is so, it must be equally true that if people vulnerable to crime are prepared and entitled to defend themselves and their property it would reduce the risk of an attack from the criminal. Even though the British public should not, as the American public is, be allowed to carry firearms, there seems to be no justification for denying citizens the right to defend themselves and their property with any object or weapon that readily comes to hand, particularly when an unauthorized person breaks into and enters their home for the purpose of crime.

Equally, the state is under an obligation to arrange machinery for settling disputes and controversies between citizens that do not culminate in violence or crime. Courts should be provided before which any person who feels aggrieved under the law or otherwise can have their grievances aired and if necessary remedied without having to seek redress by force. There should be courts to deal with family matters; the law of property and all laws relating thereto; commercial law; the law of trusts; contracts and torts; and all manner of other civil proceedings. Not only should such courts be accessible to all, but they should provide an equitable and expeditious means of remedying the position. The civil courts of England and Wales fulfil the first two purposes, but fail miserably because of the long delays that occur in arranging for the hearing of such matters.

To enable it to maintain law and order within its boundaries, the state has the monopoly of the legitimate use of physical force within its territory and the persons in the state on whom the exercise of that authority devolves compose the government of the day. Consequently, the government enjoys the supreme power in society, and individuals, owners of property and officials of private organizations for example cannot in principle use force to sustain their control but must rely upon the coercive power of the state to protect their rights. However, whatever machinery of law is provided by a liberal democratic state to ensure order within the community, it cannot function satisfactorily unless there is some consensus in society concerning the laws, the principles behind them and the system of application. Only if (as in Aldous Huxley's *Brave New World*) men were rigorously conditioned as embryos for their future social roles could conformity be complete; but this can never be so. However, some measure of conformity is clearly a prerequisite of an ordered society and this is achieved because generally people want to obey the laws and mores of their society for various reasons.

The main non-coercive pressures towards conformity are internal; they are acquired and encouraged during the process of socialization, which in modern societies takes place mainly in the family, peer group and school. In this process the keeping of rules, laws and mores is transformed into habit, socially approved aims into ambitions and social values into a self-regulating conscience. Individuals are encouraged not to break rules and regulations, and they begin to feel that it is 'right' and beneficial if they do not do so. But the tendencies towards conformity resulting from socialization do not lead to a complete mechanical acquiescence to the laws and cultural demands. Personal gratification and social requirements are often at odds, and even the most thorough process of socialization is not likely to subdue private impulses completely. Society often requires behaviour that is unpleasant, difficult and irksome to some individuals and therefore to be avoided if possible. However, the tendency towards deviant behaviour must in some degree be contained. Despite all the mechanisms that elicit or enforce conformity, no community is ever totally free from some disregard of its standards of propriety and the deviations vary from the mild peccadilloes of most people to murder and treason by the few.

From a psychological point of view, the origins of deviant behaviour are said to lie in the personality, namely in unsatisfied needs, unmanageable duties or emotional problems, but psychological interpretations of criminal behaviour need not rest upon instincts or innate tendencies. Indeed, individuals may come to ignore the dictates of society because of their particular social experience. Parent neglect, excessive demands upon the child or a continuing conflict between parent and child may for example lead to psychological tendencies that encourage rejection or disregard for laws and regulations. Therefore, because early experience is particularly important in the formation of traits, nonconformity frequently seems to reflect the failure of socialization. It may be due to the parents' unwillingness or inability to inculcate respect for others or for prevailing social values, or to their stimulation of aggressive or hostile feelings. Indeed, parents may even transmit socially objectionable habits or interests to the child directly. Thus most forms of deviant behaviour are rarely distributed equally throughout all sections of society. Vehicle thefts, robbery and assault are more frequent in the lower sections of society. Delinquent juvenile gangs are mainly, although not completely, a phenomenon of high-density urban residential areas. Researchers of crime and delinquency have often noted the existence of sub-cultures that educate and sustain the legal offender, both adult and juvenile. The importance of the sub-culture is indicated by the fact that only about one fifth of juvenile offenders acts alone. The great majority carry on their activities with others who hold similar attitudes and values.

Law-abiding citizens may have impulses that could lead to crime, but they have not had the opportunities to learn the necessary skills or to develop the appropriate attitudes and sentiments. Although the process of transmission by which deviant habits, opinions, knowledge and values are passed on to receptive neophytes sheds considerable light on the origins of deviant behaviour, it demonstrates that not all deviant behaviour can be traced to a deviant sub-culture. For example, crimes of passion and crimes of embezzlement and fraud are often committed by individuals with little or no contact with other offenders and no prior knowledge of criminal folkways.

It follows that crime will always exist in society, but it should be contained and limited to a small criminal minority in the total population. Currently there is a threat to the general structure of society because of certain juvenile activities of the sort which become popular and fashionable from time to time, some throughout the entire class structure, others at certain social levels or in certain geographical areas. These may involve criminal activities such as shoplifting, mugging the aged, smoking marijuana or other drugs, and including 'glue-sniffing'. Schoolboys are frequently ridiculed by their friends for refusing to participate in the 'game', and unless the socializing process of families and schools has been internalized the young person may be gradually absorbed into a deviant role and become identified as a criminal or drug addict.

Unfortunately large numbers of families, although well intentioned, have failed in their duty to socialize their children. Over the years certain psychological theories have implied that children should not be denied full 'free expression' and that correction was taboo. Such ideas have been widely publicized and accepted by the influential avant garde, which led to their acceptance by a substantial number of parents. Some parents' natural reactions prevented them from adopting the theories in practice because they involuntarily corrected their children when they misbehaved. It appears that those parents who accepted the theories and were capable of implementing them deprived their children of the natural process of socialization and left them a disturbing influence at school and prone to the popular and fashionable sub-cultures of the young. Even worse, the parents of such children often object to school discipline being exercised, making it impossible for the teachers to undertake the parents' duty to socialize the child. On the other hand, experience has shown that the theories have given very many parents an excuse to ignore their responsibilities and duties to socialize their children and they leave it entirely to the school teachers to do so. Although the school teachers do their best, alone they are unable completely to socialize their pupils, particularly as schools are not financed or arranged to give moral instruction and are often powerless to discipline the recalcitrant youngster. Very often if complaints are made to the parents concerning the conduct of their children, the complainants are either met with abuse or they are referred to the police because the parents are unable to discipline their own children.

The law relating to this matter appears to be self-destructive, because if eventually a young person gets beyond parental control and therefore persuasion, scolding and sanctions are of no avail, the parents cannot, in an effort to prevent a repetition of their son's or daughter's wrong doings, resort to moderate corporal punishment without the risk of being charged for assault. In instances where a parent has contravened this law, some youngsters have reported that parent to the police. If any relative in the extended family administered a sharp physical admonishment to a young person for a flagrant breach of reasonable conduct, that relative could be charged with assault. A school teacher who has his or her class disrupted by one or more unruly pupils, preventing a further twenty or so pupils from being educated, can take no physical remedies against those unruly pupils, even if all other remedies available to them have failed. If a motorist witnesses someone daubing his car with paint or removing parts of the car, he cannot give the offender 'a cuff' to prevent further damage without the risk of proceedings for assault being instituted. This risk is accepted by most of the law-abiding citizens and consequently the law is more often ignored than observed, though it is not ignored by the police.

When a youngster's conduct has been more serious, the police themselves cannot legally admonish the offender, they can only refer the matter to the juvenile court, where offenders in the main are dealt with so leniently that they often walk from the court – amused with the proceedings and calling their police accusers 'pigs' to their face. After repeatedly being brought before the juvenile court, they eventually receive custodial sentences, but by that time the die is cast and in those establishments to which they are committed they join the more advanced deviant groups which equip them with the knowledge and sentiments for a life of criminal activity.

12

INTERNATIONAL LAW

Silent enim leges inter arma.

CICERO, *Pro Milone* (52 BC)

A review of the laws of England and Wales and their practical application cannot be satisfactorily concluded without examining the effect of international law upon Britain and its inhabitants and in particular the laws of the European Economic Community, which are imposed upon all member states and every citizen of those states. In doing so it is important to bear in mind that the salient difference between national law and international law is that national law, in the normal course of events, functions in an established legal system, and national authorities have a monopoly of sufficient legitimate power to enforce the laws. There is, however, no monopoly of legitimate power to enforce international law and, while accepting the existence of treaties between certain nations, many people have questioned whether in fact there is such a thing as international law in the context of the worldwide arena.

The reports of early explorers and more recently anthropological studies have noted the sophisticated rules and ceremonies which were associated with economic, diplomatic and military transactions between tribes, lineage groups, city states and ancient empires. Almost all peoples used forms of treaties to secure peace, followed by some kind of ceremony, ritual or sacrifice to seal obligations. The sanctions to those treaties were very often religious beliefs that those who broke them would die or receive some violent punishment. But peacemaking could not take place without the recognition of the inviolability of a belligerent tribe's representatives or of some mediating third party. Various forms of diplomatic immunities were extended to all kinds of messengers and envoys in those primitive systems, not just those on official peace-making missions. Economic exchanges were normally carried out according to strict rules, and in many cases tribes also possessed rules and customs regulating the outbreak and the conduct of warfare. Regular observance of these religious and other restraints presupposes that the social or political units involved existed within a common civilization or culture. Indeed, in many common civilizations there were religious and other principles to be found which established routines for handling communications between political units, commercial transactions, the conduct of warfare and the observance of treaties. These placed obligations upon the decisions of policy-makers, and any obligation was a limitation on a government's freedom of action. Some of these obligations defined what the political units might or might not do and others pointed to what political units should not do. Clearly if political units in their foreign policy met these obligations, even at the expense of their own interests or at the expense of the efficient conduct of diplomacy or warfare, it is reasonable to infer that legal considerations, at least in part, explain their decision to do so.

These rules or laws that existed among political units of a particular culture were rarely applied in relations with 'barbarians' beyond the geographical and cultural boundaries of the system. It seems that, until the twentieth century, the Europeans, much as the Hindus, Greeks and Moslems of earlier ages, did not consider that the legal obligations observed in relations within their own culture could be applied equally in transactions with 'savages' or 'barbarians' of entirely different cultures. The order that existed in medieval Europe grew out of the authority of the Church in prescribing general rules of conduct and a tradition of 'natural law and order' from Rome, from which the principles relating to transactions between political units were developed. The Church, with its notions of hierarchy, authority and duty and its ultimate sanction of excommunication, held the power to moderate political actions of the time. The Peace of God, declared by the Church in the tenth century, imposed restrictions on war, violence and plundering, but it was unsuccessful because some political units considered certain values and interests to be more important than religious sanctions. Consequently, they interpreted the rules in an arbitrary manner or violated their obligations.

The Truce of God, established in 1041 by the Bishop of Arles and the Abbot of Cluny, was more successful and limited the area and the extent of violence in parts of medieval Europe. There was to be no fighting between Wednesday evening and Monday morning. But such declaratory laws were never observed with precision and they gained acceptance only in limited localities. Later the medieval concept of 'just war' was introduced and helped to deter some forms of violence. The Church considered war 'illegal' and its perpetrators subject to ecclesiastic punishment if it was not properly declared by established authorities, with just causes and legitimate objectives.

The concepts of sovereignty, territorial integrity, equality and non-interference in the state's internal affairs, central to modern international law, developed with the appearance of the European nation state, which no longer accepted the command of any authority outside its boundaries. Diplomats and dynasts accepted certain principles of justice derived from the 'law of nature', but generally their internal actions were restrained only by obligations undertaken with each other in treaties. Religious principles and the Church no longer limited what the new political units of kings and princes could or could not do towards their neighbouring states. What restraints existed were in the main voluntarily imposed or enforced by the threat of counter-action and retaliation. Tradition also played an important role in distinguishing between legitimate and illegitimate policies. However, claims by kings and princes that certain customs were so well established as to be part of international law rarely met with the agreement of other states, so that by the eighteenth century no legal norms existed prescribing rights and duties in international relationships nor was there a general practice of observing treaties or conducting diplomatic relations. The rules that did exist were more evident in the conduct of warfare and seemed to have come about more from the crude military technology of the day than from commonly recognized legal principles or humanitarian sentiments. Nevertheless, jurists and diplomats continued to elaborate on the 'law of nations', the number of international treaties proliferated and state rulers increasingly referred to legal advisers in conducting their policies, though they did not always apply the advice they received.

At the end of the eighteenth century, the increasing amount of European inter-state trade and the development of sources of raw materials and markets in non-European areas provided the European states with similar outlooks and objectives. These required rules to place transactions and economic relations on a stable and predictable basis. Britain's dominant naval position in the nineteenth century enabled it to establish the foundations for the modern law of the sea. Although its aims to regulate maritime commerce during peace and war were designed to serve British private and public interests, they happened to coincide, in many instances, with the interests of other states as well. The greatest proliferation of legal doctrines related to the obligations of debtor states, the sanctity of money, the protection of commercial property during civil strife and the expropriation of private property. They reflected the *laissez faire* economics and the mutual interests of European businessmen in expanding markets and obtaining security for investments. Multilateral treaties established legal control over the main waterways of the world, including the Declaration of Paris on marine law (1856), the Conventions regulating the Turkish Straits, Black Sea and Baltic Sounds and the new canals of Panama (1888) and Suez (1903). These regulations and obligations furthered the orderly expansion of commercial transactions, which were constantly increasing, but in regulating the use of force in the international arena and in moderating the national and imperial rivalries the law was far less effective. State governments viewed the threat of force as a legitimate exercise of the sovereign state's will and there was a common belief that war was a justified method of inducement.

In nineteenth-century Europe, international law began to incorporate limitations on the scope and degree of violence. New laws of neutrality established rights and obligations for both belligerents and neutrals that prevented the extension of warfare between two or more states into regional or continental holocausts. Certain areas or countries, such as Switzerland in 1815, Belgium in 1831 and the Congo basin in 1885, were permanently neutralized by the great powers, thereby removing them from involvement in conflicts. A series of multilateral conventions and codes was drafted in an attempt to prevent undue suffering among troops and civilians, with varying degrees of success. However, in most cases the laws of neutrality and warfare were observed until developments in military technology in the twentieth century made them more or less obsolete.

In order to appreciate the reasons why ordinary state governments, in the absence of any policing of the law, did not arbitrarily interpret or violate the law for short-term gain, it is necessary to examine the advantages they derived in complying with international norms. Rules simplifying procedures between governments are long-term advantages to all, in that there is an expectancy of reciprocity. In other words, a government accepts the obligations and restrictions imposed by the law or legal norms because it expects or hopes that other nation states it is in relationship with will base their decisions and responses on similar legal criteria. This discourages considerations of expediency, military 'necessity' and short-term political advantages. In time, when the advantages of law observation become clear and persistent, a habit or custom of conducting transactions according to the laws and legal norms may arise.

In addition, by observing the law, a nation state may raise its international prestige and increase diplomatic influence with other states as it develops a reputation in the international community for being 'law-abiding'. A reputation of complying with treaty and other obligations becomes an important matter in diplomatic encounters. Minor states have greater influence and have favourable consideration from major powers if they have built for themselves a reputation for observing legal obligations. If, on the other hand, the state persistently breaks treaties, and defies or capriciously misinterprets accepted international legal doctrines, its credibility in diplomatic negotiations and hence its influence is reduced. Perhaps the most important factor in persuading a nation to comply with the rules is the fear of negative sanctions or of various forms of reprisal. It was common among the new sovereign states of Europe not to accord immunities to foreign diplomats, with the result that occasionally foreign diplomats were abused, imprisoned and even executed by the government to which they were accredited. But this practice could not prevail for very long, because it was soon realized that their own representatives abroad could be, and often were, treated in a similar manner.

Although history reveals that at all times there have been those nation states that have not been prepared to accept the limitations of legal norms on their activities, the vast majority require stability and predictability in their external relationships. Indeed, if transactions between states were totally unpredictable because international laws were ignored, chaos would ensue and orderly international relationships would be impossible. To avoid this the vast majority of sovereign states have always placed a high value on at least appearing to comply with the rules, legal doctrines and treaties, and in so doing they not only displayed concern over their prestige or the possibility of retaliation but also belief in the ethical value of law observance.

International law, based on these European origins, continued to develop throughout the nineteenth and twentieth centuries despite the two world wars. It was evolved, in many cases, from what were originally customary practices and many were encapsulated into multi-lateral treaties and codes. In novel circumstances, immediate agreements were necessary between sovereign states, and instead of waiting for customs to be established, treaties were drafted, changed and adapted to particular needs. Although these treaties established new principles, rights and obligations to regulate the relationships between the states who were signatories to the treaties, they could not establish new rights or obligations for those states that were not parties to them. On the other hand, customary rules of law could be invoked by all states. The nineteenth-century attitude towards and doctrine of war as an instrument of policy to be declared by any government solely on its own discretion was abandoned, and international law sought not only to regulate, stabilize and make predictable types and quantities of commercial and political transactions that were mainly unprecedented but to reflect new ethical values that condemned the use of force as an instrument of inducement. The more formal attempts to regulate the use of force resulted in the League of Nations Covenant, the Geneva Protocol of 1924, the Treaty for the Renunciation of War (the Kellog-Brand Treaty, 1928), the Anti-War Treaty of Rio de Janeiro in 1933 and finally the United Nations Charter. Some of these treaties and charters are not entirely clear in their details and, as some of the provisions have been manipulated, the use of force has not yet been effectively regulated. It is now more likely for an invading force to claim that it had been invited in by a legitimate government to restore law and order or adopt some other device in an attempt to avoid having to face widespread criticism. But international law is not an arbitrary set of rules. The provisions of the United Nations Charter prohibiting the threat or the use of force, or the principles of the Genocide Convention, emanate directly from un-written understandings and from the widespread belief that the use of force or the systematic slaying of religious or ethnic groups is inherently immoral and ethically reprehensible.

Although a body of international law has been evolving there are not and never have been effective institutional judicial mechanisms to enforce that law. Prior to the development of the nation state, when Europe was carved into a patchwork of duchies, free city states, monarchies and principalities mediation services were often available involving the Church and sometimes even the Pope himself. This order was destroyed on the emergence of the sovereign state, which recognized no authority outside its boundaries over its internal or external affairs. However, in later centuries, a number of states entered into treaties that required the arbitration of disputes, and at the end of the nineteenth century, because of the success of arbitration, a number of states agitated for permanent international institutions to handle inter-state conflicts and disputes. It was argued that the establishment of a permanent international tribunal, armed with enforcement powers and supported by limitations on armaments, could herald an era of peace.

These arguments influenced some governments, and in 1899 and 1907 international conferences were instituted at The Hague to discuss plans for such institutions. The outcome was the General Act for the Pacific Settlement of International Disputes, to which fifty states eventually adhered. The delegates also drafted a Convention establishing the Permanent Court of Arbitration, which was in fact neither permanent nor a court, but a list of arbitrators (nominated by members of the Convention) who could be selected by the parties to a dispute to decide a particular case. Article 38 of the General Act urged the signatories to use arbitral procedures for questions of international contentions, but it exempted states from submitting disputes or conflicts involving questions of 'national honour'. Thus the arrangements provided an inadequate basis for the court's jurisdiction and failed to provide it with means of enforcing the decisions it made. In addition the submission of cases to arbitral procedures was based on the principle of voluntarism.

The creation of the League of Nations brought with it the most far-reaching innovation in procedures for the pacific resolution of international conflicts, as well as disputes. The major new principle of the League's Covenant was that the international community had not only the right but a duty to intervene in international conflicts and that parties to a conflict or dispute had the obligation to submit their differences to some procedure ranging from bilateral negotiations to submitting their case to the Permanent Court of International Justice. Under Article 16, to prevent non-compliance with its decision, the Council was empowered to order economic and military sanctions if any member should resort to war in disregard of the terms of the Articles of the Covenant. All members of the League were to consider the use of force in violation of the Articles as an attack on themselves. While these provisions were designed to deter aggression and assure compliance with all decisions in the various settlement procedures, the history of the League in fulfilling those commitments was disappointing. In 1923 the Canadians sponsored a resolution which reserved for each member of the League the decision whether or not aggression had occurred and whether or not each member state should apply sanctions. Although the resolution was not passed, the vast majority of the member states indicated that they were in favour of it. Thus the League was deprived of whatever right it had under the Covenant to undertake action on its own authority. This was apparent between 1923 and 1939, when European governments showed repeatedly that they rather than the League or the Permanent Court of International Justice would decide what actions would have to be taken against the aggressions by major powers, and the Second World War demonstrated the extent to which states ignored international law and conventions, thus confirming, in a rather different context, Cicero's comment quoted at the start of the chapter, the translation of which is 'Laws are inoperative in war'.

After the Second World War the United Nations Charter attempted to set up a peace-keeping organization that avoided the pitfalls experienced by the League of Nations, and the International Court of Justice succeeded the Permanent Court of International Justice. The United Nations Charter provided various means of resolving conflicts, but the final procedure was adjudication whereby the parties, by prior agreement, could submit issues under contention to an independent legal tribunal.

The Court would decide the case on the basis of international law, and its jurisdiction extends only to legal issues. According to the optional clause of the Statute of the International Court of Justice, a legal issue is loosely defined as the interpretation of a treaty; any question of international law; the existence of any fact that, if established, would constitute a breach of an international obligation; and the nature or extent of the reparation to be made for the breach of an international obligation. The record of the International Court of Justice has been dismal, because a government that knows or feels that it has only a weak legal position in a contentious situation will not agree to this method of resolution, since under it there can be only a winner and a loser. Compromise, which is central to diplomatic bargaining and mediation, cannot be the result of judicial proceedings. Moreover, the cases that have come before international tribunals reveal that the parties have disagreed primarily over the establishment of facts or the meaning of existing laws or treaties. In most international conflicts, one of the parties is attempting to change the other's rights, privileges or obligations. Thus, although most conflicts have important legal aspects, one or both of the parties do not wish to define their positions in legal terms because their political objectives and actions are clearly incompatible with existing legal principles or jurisdictions. In other words, the dispute has become too deeply embroiled in, or is symbolic of, greater tensions and conflicts between the two or more states.

Finally, there is the problem of the sources of modern international law, and governmental attitudes towards that law. Many existing legal principles were developed to help regulate the jurisdictions, forms of interactions, and responsibilities of the European states during the eighteenth and nineteenth centuries. Some principles were designed specifically to protect European commercial interests and colonial relationships. Aside from most communist governments, which have rejected some doctrines of 'western' international law, legal scholars have noted that a lot of the new states are less than enthusiastic about many of those older principles. They have numerous economic, political and commercial needs that cannot be regulated effectively, or which cannot be met, by the application of the older norms. Hence, the reluctance of many of the new states or nations to accept the compulsory jurisdiction of the International Court of Justice may be explained by the suspicion towards the former colonial powers and the legal principles that they developed to take care of their own needs. Indeed experience has shown that 'open' states are more likely to utilize the International Court of Justice than 'closed' states and that 'developed' states were three times more likely to use the court than 'undeveloped' states or 'intermediate' states.

In terms of power of the contestants, research has shown that in cases submitted to the courts, the initiator is usually the stronger of the two states involved in the conflict or dispute. The weakness of the system is that the International Courts have always been powerless – powerless to order any state to appear before it and powerless to enforce any judgment it may deliver. Unlike those of the old European international system, the people who make decisions on international events today do so on a basis of diverse traditions, ideologies and ethical standards. With such diverse values, and therefore perceptions, not only may the people in question differ as to what constitutes moral or immoral behaviour, but the meaning they ascribe to a set of commonly perceived facts may be so diverse as to preclude development of any common worldwide legal opinion on a situation.

While the International Courts could not obtain the collaboration of all states and the use of force continued to be unregulated throughout the world, in Europe greater economic cooperation drew the countries closer together in their attempt to reconstruct their devastated cities and rebuild their economic base. The European Coal and Steel Community was initiated by Belgium, France, Germany, Luxembourg and the Netherlands in 1951, and this purely functional economic arrangement gave hopes of closer cooperation between the member states by the foundation of a wider and deeper community. That intention took a major step forward in 1957, when the six states agreed to establish Euratom, another functional institution, and the much broader and potentially political European Economic Community.

Although, at that time, Britain was invited to join the developments, the British were initially sceptical of the ability of the Europeans, who had previously been constantly in conflict with each other, to work together closely. At the same time the British economy was healthier than those of the continental states that had been ravaged by war, and the British felt that they were not only the strongest state in Europe but they held an important place, as a great power, in international affairs. There may well have been a certain degree of justification for the point of view. Although in the 1950s Britain could not rival the armed might of the United States of America or the

Union of Soviet Socialist Republics, she was the third most powerful state, with what she considered to be a 'special relationship' with the United States and Commonwealth links that spanned the world. Moreover, at that time, the majority of the British people eyed all foreigners, especially those on the other side of the Channel, with a degree of suspicion. Thus in the 1950s British hopes for western Europe were centred on its economic recovery, which involved cooperation between France and Germany, the traditional European belligerents, and a reduction in threat of further wars on the continent. Indeed, the Treaty of Rome included political and legal considerations that involved a reduction in formal state sovereignty that Britain was not prepared to sacrifice.

However, Britain's economic position in the world and its international influence rapidly deteriorated. In a speech in the House of Commons on 31 July 1961 Harold Macmillan, the Prime Minister, said: 'The future relations between the European Economic Community, the United Kingdom, the Commonwealth and the rest of Europe are clearly matters of capital importance in the life of our country and, indeed, of all countries of the free world. This is a political as well as an economic issue. Although the Treaty of Rome is concerned with economic matters, it has an important political objective, namely to promote unity and stability in Europe which is so essential a factor in a struggle for freedom and progress throughout the world. In this modern world the tendency towards larger groups of nations acting together in common interest leads to greater unity and thus adds strength. I believe that it is both our duty and our interest to contribute towards that strength by securing the closest possible unity with Europe.'

Britain formally entered the European Economic Community in 1973 and in addition to the worldwide international laws and the treaties and conventions it had to adhere to, it became subject to the narrow range of European law and subject to the primacy of the Community's Court of Justice in relation to that law.

Lawmaking in the Community is far removed from lawmaking in the British Parliament. There are five institutions of the Community that are directly or indirectly involved in the lawmaking process, but the European Parliament, comprising the elected representatives of the member states, acts in a consultative and advisory capacity with the executive Commission and the Council of Ministers and has no direct participation in the lawmaking. The Commission is comprised of technical experts appointed by common agreement among the member states' governments, and they are responsible to the organization only. They may initiate policy recommendations, frame the necessary rules, regulations and directives, and administer those that have been approved by the member governments. Members of the Commission also sit in all meetings of the Council of Ministers and represent the viewpoint of the Community. The Council of Ministers is attended by national representatives, and has the final authority to formulate and approve laws and common policies and in the process bargain among themselves. The Council of Ministers is assisted by the Committee of Permanent Representatives. Finally, the Court of Justice of the Community reviews the legality of the decisions of the Commission and the Council of Ministers and hears legal cases arising under the founding treaties. It considers conflicts brought by governments against each other, conflicts between governments and the Commission and actions by individuals or business enterprises against the Commission or against member states. (The formal structure is shown in Appendix 4.)

The pattern of lawmaking within these institutions is complex and involves work by a large number of bureaucrats, both national and international. For instance, the Commission starts to plan rules, regulations and directives to give effect to the goals of economic integration. In compiling the framework for the proposals, members of the Commission consult the Permanent Representatives of the member states, who report to their own governments, and naturally will consult extensively with their own bureaucrats in their national capitals. The Permanent Representatives defend national points of view, but as they are intimately connected with all the affairs of the Community, they act as advocates for the Community and often urge their own governments to support the Commission's point of view as well. When the long process of consultation, which may or may not involve the European Parliament, is completed and a coherent set of proposals emerge, the Commission presents them to the Council of Ministers, comprising the Foreign, Economics, Finance and Trade Ministers, of the member states. The Commission sits in the Council as an additional member, except that it represents the viewpoint of the Community, not that of a member state. It can argue in favour of its proposals, make new proposals, or act as a mediator should some Ministers find themselves in deadlock.

Voting in the Council of Ministers is complicated, but for the purpose of this work suffice it to say that most decisions of the Council can be taken against the will of one or more of the member state governments, although the informal 'code' of operation in the Council requires the Ministers to reach an agreement acceptable to all. Therefore most directives and regulations of the Community are made through the slow and difficult process of arriving at an overall consensus through persuasion, presentation of evidence and the production of all necessary documentation. Of course, most proposals reaching the Council of Ministers involve losses and gains for various member states and each Minister will naturally attempt to ensure that the final decision reflects the interests of his national government to the maximum extent possible. However, the negotiations in the Council of Ministers start with an implicit understanding that a decision must be finally arrived at so as to exclude the possibility of not reaching an agreement at all, and this assumes that mutual concessions must be made. In the lengthy discussions the Commission, an in-built mediator, is always present and constantly represents the views of the Community. Because it is armed with technical expertise and legitimacy, it is in a powerful position to influence the bargaining positions of the member states. The Ministers are more likely to make concessions, and to justify those concessions to their national governments, if they are made in the name of the Community rather than in favour of another member state. The Commission is therefore in a strong position to overcome strictly national imperatives.

Most issues in the institutional framework of the Community are dealt with as 'problems' and solutions can be based on data, the elucidation of needs and the application of technology. Ideological principles very rarely reveal themselves in the bargaining that takes place within the Council of Ministers, or between the Commission and the Permanent Representatives. Thus the decisions and 'solutions' are based not on power, prestige, capabilities or reputations of member states but on the objectives of the organizations and the most convincing needs of its members. It makes little difference that Luxembourg is geographically minuscule compared with France or

Germany or militarily weak compared with Britain. In the Council, French Ministers have often reduced their demands to accommodate the Netherlands, while on other issues the Germans have retreated from their bargaining positions to placate the Belgians. No national government, therefore, consistently gains or withdraws from its objective on the sole basis that it is economically or militarily weak or strong. The Ministers display considerable sensitivity towards the needs of other member states with the awareness that they are working on a common problem, one in which compromise is expected from all sides in order to obtain a Community solution. If, after all efforts, an agreement cannot be arrived at, the proposals or projects are normally returned to the Commission for reworking. The Commission then re-establishes contact with the Permanent Representatives, or with national bureaucrats, and irons out the remaining problems.

There have been disruptions in the procedure, notably those brought about at the instigation of France under General de Gaulle, but they have been temporary. Generally, the repeated exposure to bargaining sessions of the nature described, and the many successful outcomes that have resulted from them, have undoubtedly built up personal commitments among the Ministers, but it must be re-membered that those problems of the European Community are con-cerned primarily with economic questions, involving issues where technical factors and information can be used to influence negotiators. It is not directly concerned with incompatible ideological values, long-range objectives, territorial claims or more diffuse national aspi-rations and no criteria for agreement on these matters exist. Even so, the continual effort to unify the law of all member states relating to economic matters is a herculean task because the laws of the individual member states are rooted in different origins. For instance, while British law has evolved under the influence of ancient Roman law, French law is based on the Napoleonic Code and there is one funda-mental difference between them in the commercial sphere that pre-vents any unification of law, particularly in the area of insolvency. In British law, unless there is any agreement to the contrary, when a person or commercial undertaking agrees to purchase goods but pay-ment is not immediately made, the ownership of the goods passes to the purchaser forthwith and the seller's remedy against the purchaser is to claim payment for the goods. In French law, ownership of goods remains with the seller until the goods have been paid for. Many other variances exist throughout the legal systems of the member states, so that Community law emanating from the Commission and the Council of Ministers is in the form of directives and regulations. When possible the law is framed as a regulation that has the force of national law in all member states, but when that is not possible it is in the form of a directive that is binding as an objective on all member states. Both regulations and directives are administered under the primacy of the Community Court of Justice.

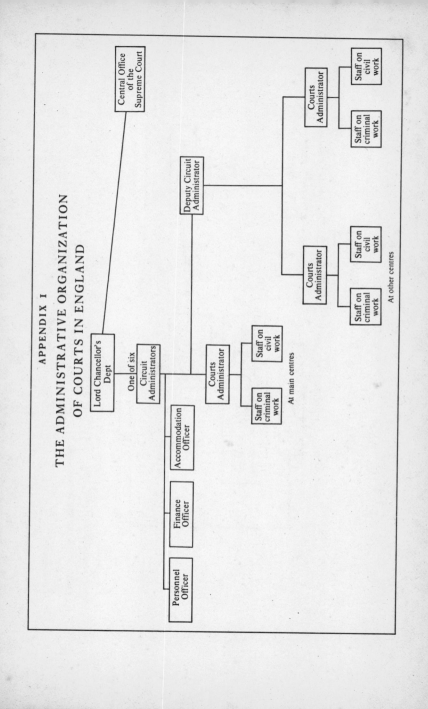

APPENDIX I

THE ADMINISTRATIVE ORGANIZATION
OF COURTS IN ENGLAND

Lord Chancellor's Dept ── Central Office of the Supreme Court

Personnel Officer · Finance Officer · Accommodation Officer

One of six Circuit Administrators

Deputy Circuit Administrator

Courts Administrator — Staff on criminal work / Staff on civil work (At main centres)

Courts Administrator — Staff on criminal work / Staff on civil work
Courts Administrator — Staff on criminal work / Staff on civil work
At other centres

APPENDIX 2

THE COURT SYSTEM IN ENGLAND

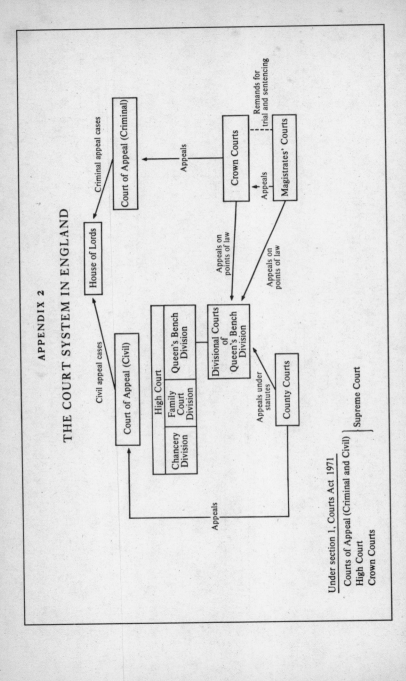

Under section 1, Courts Act 1971

Courts of Appeal (Criminal and Civil) ⎤
High Court   ⎬ Supreme Court
Crown Courts   ⎦

APPENDIX 3

THE FORMAL STRUCTURE OF LAW COURTS IN THE UNITED STATES OF AMERICA

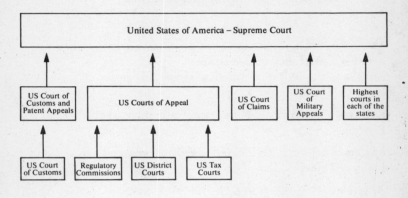

APPENDIX 4

THE FORMAL STRUCTURE OF THE EUROPEAN ECONOMIC COMMUNITY'S LAWMAKING PROCESS

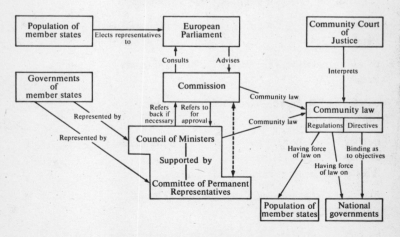

SELECT BIBLIOGRAPHY

ABEL-SMITH, B., and STEVENS, R. (1967), *Lawyers and the Courts*, London: Heinemann.

ABEL-SMITH, B., and STEVENS, R. (1968), *In Search of Justice*, London: Allen Lane.

AUBERT, V. (1969), *Sociology of Law*, Harmondsworth: Penguin.

BARTON, M. (1964), *The Policeman in the Community*, London: Tavistock.

Britain 1984, An Official Handbook, HM Stationery Office, prepared by the Central Office of Information.

CHAPMAN, D. (1968), *Sociology and the Stereotype of the Criminal*, London: Tavistock.

CHURCHWARD, L. G. (1975), *Contemporary Soviet Government*, London: Routledge & Kegan Paul.

COHEN, S. (1971), *Images of Deviance*, Harmondsworth: Penguin.

DEVLIN, P. (1979), *The Judge*, Oxford University Press.

DIAS, R. W. M. (1970), *Jurisprudence*, London: Butterworth.

DICEY, A. V. (1905), *Lectures on the Relation Between Law and Public Opinion in England During the Nineteenth Century*, London: Macmillan.

DU CANN, C. G. L. (1960), *Miscarriages of Justice*, London: Muller.

FRANKS, LORD (1957), *Report of the Committee on*

Administrative Tribunals and Enquiries, Cmnd 218, London: HMSO.

HANSON, A. H., and WALLES, M. (1970), *Governing Britain*, London: Fontana.

HOEBEL, E. A. (1954), *The Law of Primitive Man*, Cambridge, Mass.: Harvard University Press.

HOLSTI, K. J. (1973), *International Politics*, New Jersey: Prentice-Hall.

JACKSON, R. M. (1967), *The Machinery of Justice in England and Wales*: Cambridge University Press.

JENKS, E. (1949), *Book of English Law*, London: John Murray.

LASKI, H. (1932), *Studies in Law and Politics*, London: Allen & Unwin.

MCDONALD, L. (1969), *Delinquency and Social Class*, London: Faber.

MACMILLAN, H. (1972), *Pointing the Way 1959–61*, Basingstoke: Macmillan.

MANCHESTER, A. H., *Modern Legal History*, London: Butterworth.

MARSHALL, G. (1967), *Police and Government*, London: Methuen.

SALMOND, J. W. (1966), *Jurisprudence*, London: Sweet & Maxwell.

INDEX